VAN HELSING
THE MAKING OF THE LEGEND

Foreword and Screenplay by STEPHEN SOMMERS

Edited by LINDA SUNSHINE   Design by TIMOTHY SHANER

A NEWMARKET PICTORIAL MOVIEBOOK

NEWMARKET PRESS • NEW YORK

This book is published in the United States of America.

FIRST EDITION

10 9 8 7 6 5 4 3 2 1   10 9 8 7 6 5 4 3 2 1
1-55704-628-X (Paperback)   1-55704-629-8 (Hardcover)

Library of Congress Cataloging-in-Publication Data available upon request.

QUANTITY PURCHASES
Companies, professional groups, clubs, and other organizations may qualify for special terms when ordering quantities of this title. For information, write Special Sales Department, Newmarket Press, 18 East 48th Street, New York, NY 10017; call (212) 832-3575; fax (212) 832-3629; or e-mail mailbox@newmarketpress.com.

www.newmarketpress.com

Designed by Timothy Shaner

Manufactured in the United States of America.

OTHER NEWMARKET PICTORIAL MOVIEBOOKS INCLUDE:

Contents

FOREWORD

By Stephen Sommers

After writing and directing *The Mummy* and *The Mummy Returns*, two very large, very complex movies, I decided I wanted to do a small movie, an uncomplicated movie, maybe a movie about two people chatting on a beach. So I sat at my computer…and then I paced around my office…and then I sat at my computer again…this went on for days. Two people chatting on a beach is not a very interesting idea. And then I thought, but what if Dracula showed up, that would be interesting. And then what if Frankenstein's Monster arrived? That would be a nice twist. And surely, if I had those two, I couldn't leave out The Wolf Man. What a triumvirate that would be. And while I'm at it, let's replace one of those two boring people just sitting on the beach with a man who works for an ancient secret society based under the Vatican, trained by monks and mullahs from Tibet to Istanbul, whose life, job, curse, is to vanquish evil. And then let's replace the girl on the beach with an Eastern European Princess whose family has been fighting Dracula and his minions for more than four hundred years. And about that beach? I mean, I could get a sunburn filming on the beach. Sand could get in our cameras. There might be mosquitoes. Sharks live nearby. Forget the beach, let's cut the beach and replace it with some place really cool, like Transylvania. I'm not being facetious; this is how my mind works.

But I knew the movie couldn't just be about my hero taking on the three Big Guys. Anybody could come up with that idea. I needed a way in, a way to interweave all of the characters, stories, and backgrounds.

LEFT: Concept drawing of The Wolf Man.
RIGHT: Director/writer Stephen Sommers on set.

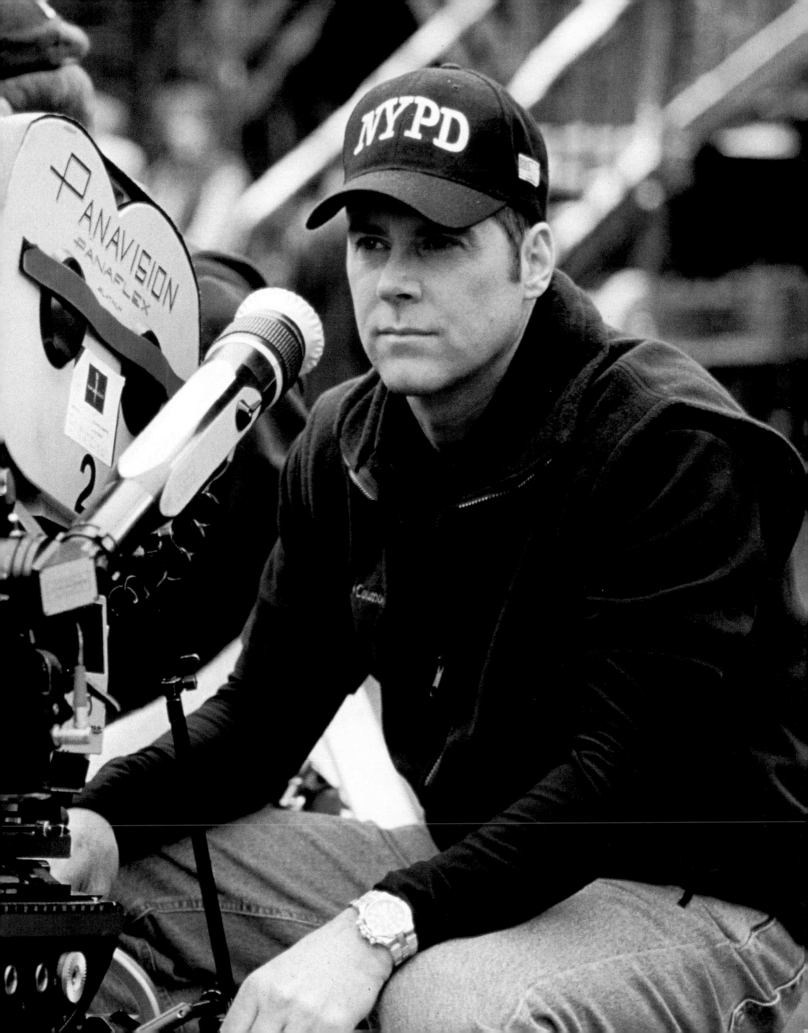

FOREWORD

I watched the three original classics again. Nowadays, most people think of *Dracula, Frankenstein* and *The Wolf Man* as horror movies, but they are actually melodramas, with very deep central characters. Frankenstein's Monster has a lot in common with Lenny in Steinbeck's *Of Mice and Men,* you feel almost as bad for him as for his victims. He's part Elephant Man, part Jud Fry from *Oklahoma!* On the other hand, The Wolf Man is more like a drug addict or alcoholic: He could be your brother, best friend, or favorite neighbor during the day, but at night, when his demons or the full moon come out, you better run for the hills. Dracula has his own difficulties: He has no heart, he feels no love, nor sorrow, nor pity. He is hollow, and he will live forever.

Now how do I connect all three of these incredibly rich characters? I did some more pacing. I did some more research. I read the books, I watched the movies, I memorized the myths, the legends, the rules. Then I started asking interesting questions. For instance, we all know that Dracula has no reflection in a mirror, but no one to my knowledge has ever asked why. I did. And in my movie I knew I needed to answer that question. I stared at my computer. Then I started thinking about Dracula and his brides. What would a man do locked up in a castle with three gorgeous women for four hundred years? I mean, in his spare time. Exactly. But vampires are the undead, so I figure their offspring, spawn, whatever, would be born dead. So what would Dracula do when, inevitably, his three brides start henpecking him to fix this situation? He would search for one of the world's premier scientists, one obsessed with reanimation, one with dubious moral character and maybe a God complex. See, I told you this is how my mind works. So, financed by Dracula, Victor Frankenstein creates the Frankenstein Monster, unwittingly making the Monster the key to life for Dracula's children. A plot is born. And so is the beginning of a movie called *Van Helsing.* Enjoy!

LEFT: Hugh Jackman and Stephen Sommers talk between takes. BELOW: Filming a close-up of Jackman and his Gatling crossbow.

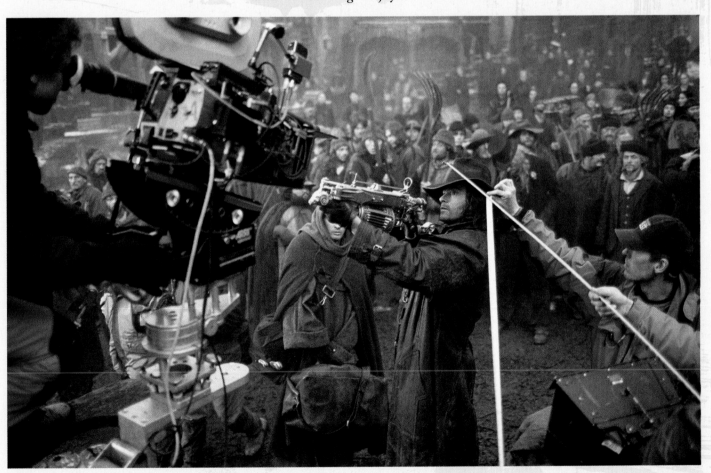

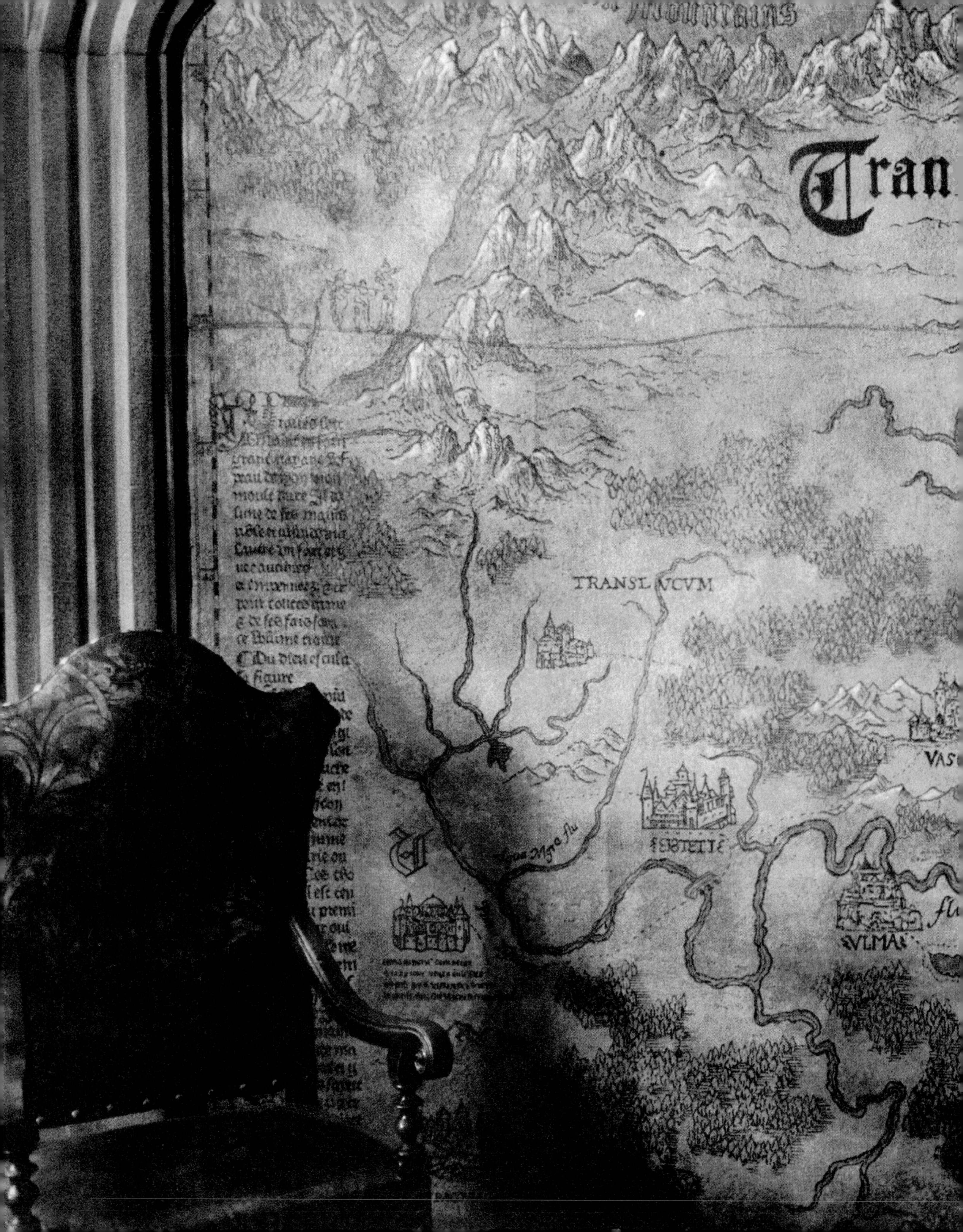
Tran
VLMA

lvania

PATAVIA

Part One

THE LEGEND LIVES

Return to Transylvania

LEFT: Frankenstein's Castle enhanced with special effects lightning.

In the 1930s, Universal Studios managed to stay profitable, in large measure, because of the unexpected success of their horror films even though the head of the studio, Carl Laemmle, disliked the genre. "I don't believe in horror pictures," Laemmle once said. "It's morbid. None of our officers are for it. People don't want that sort of thing, only Junior wanted it."

Junior was Laemmle's son and had been appointed general manager of the studio by his father in 1929, when he was twenty-one years old. After Junior successfully produced the anti-war epic *All Quiet on the Western Front*, he bought a 1927 play based on Bram Stoker's Gothic novel. Originally titled *The Un-Dead*, the book was called *Dracula* when it was published in 1897. Stoker also wrote a stage version of the story shortly before he died in 1912. His widow, Florence Stoker, kept a watchful eye on the property and promptly sued when Friedrich Wilhelm Murnau's German film *Nosferatu*, an unauthorized version of the story, appeared in 1922. The filmmakers were forced to destroy all prints of this classic Expressionist film (though prints have survived and the film is currently available on video).

An authorized version of *Dracula* opened on the London stage in the mid-1920s, was an enormous hit, and moved to Broadway in 1927. The play went on to tour the United States and Canada and was so successful that the *New York Times* noted: "Somebody will have to club *Dracula* to death if it's ever to stop."

Purchasing the movie rights from Stoker's widow was a long and complicated negotiation, but Junior persisted and finally won her over. Universal wanted Lon Chaney to portray Dracula in his first talkie, but he passed on the project and then died on August 26, 1930, just four days after Universal secured the rights to *Dracula*. Tod Browning, Chaney's favorite director, was secured for the film version of *Dracula* in an effort to entice Chaney to the title role. Browning wanted a screen actor unknown for the role and after Chaney's death turned to Bela Lugosi, the Hungarian-born actor who had played the part on Broadway. Lugosi had a chilling stage presence and voice and eventually became famous for starring in horror films.

Though Universal's first *Dracula* seems quite tame by today's standards, it was considered a radical departure in its day. Nothing like this film had ever been made in America and the studio was nervous about the public's reaction. Instead

of promoting the horror aspects of the film, it was originally marketed as a romance, of all things, and released on Valentine's Day, 1931. *Dracula* was promoted as: "The story of the strangest passion the world has ever known." Indeed.

To the surprise and delight of the studio, *Dracula* was an enormous success and, as they say in Hollywood, nothing succeeds like success. The studio rushed *Frankenstein* into production, helmed by James Whale, then the most sought-after director on the lot. Whale had made three successful war films including *Waterloo Bridge*, his first film, for Universal, and was offered whatever property he wanted for his next project. He chose *Frankenstein* because it was such a total departure for him.

The studio had wanted Lugosi for the lead role but the actor refused the part, characterizing it as "undignified" and complaining that it was a non-speaking part and that he would be unrecognizable beneath all the makeup. (He later went on, however, to play the monster in *Frankenstein Meets the Wolf Man!*) Whale was told he could choose whoever he wanted for the lead. One day in the commissary, he spotted Boris Karloff and asked if the actor wanted to play a monster. "His face fascinated me," Whale later said. "I made drawings of his head, adding sharp bony ridges where I imagined his skull might have been joined." Karloff had been working in Hollywood for ten years and admired Whale's previous work, so he agreed to take the part.

In the book *Monster Show*, author David Skal relates a story told by Karloff about the first time the actor wore his monster makeup. "When the makeup was ready for a screen test in black and white," Skal writes, "Karloff had no idea how effective the finished product would be. Would it inspire horror or laughter? Boris Karloff says, 'I was thinking this, practicing my walk, as I rounded a bend in the corridor and came face to face with this prop man. He was the first man to see the monster. I watched to study his reaction. It was quick to come. He turned white, gurgled and lunged out of sight down the corridor. Never saw him again. Poor chap. I would've liked to thank him. He was the audience that first made me feel like the monster.'"

Universal's 1931 *Frankenstein* created even more of a sensation than *Dracula*. Shot for just over $250,000, the movie grossed more than $1,000,000 in its initial release (more than twice the take from *Dracula*). Whale added many innovative flourishes. In the opening shot, for example, a gravedigger is shoveling dirt on a coffin. To get an authentic sound, Whale placed a microphone inside the coffin, a sound effect that greatly unnerved audiences when the film was released.

Universal waited four years before releasing a sequel, *Bride of Frankenstein*, starring Karloff and Elsa Lanchester as his woman. Teamed again with James Whale, the *Bride* mixed humor and horror together for the first time, creating a movie that many consider the best classic horror film of all time.

In the late 1930s and early 1940s, Karloff's career skyrocketed because of his

monster movies. Though he often railed against the typecasting, the actor also admitted, "The monster was the best friend I ever had." Whale's career, on the other hand, went in the opposite direction. Unable to work in Hollywood, he took up painting. (Whale's life and tragic suicide were chronicled in *Gods and Monsters*, a fascinating, award-winning 1998 biopic starring Ian McKellen.)

In the 1940s, Universal continued to make horror films including at least eight films featuring the Frankenstein monster, often in concert with the other classic monsters: Dracula and The Wolf Man. In addition to Karloff, Bela Lugosi and Lon Chaney Jr. had successful careers playing various monsters.

By the mid-1940s, horror movies began to fall out of favor. Some say this was because, by combining the characters, the plot lines ran out of steam. Others note that the war and other economic factors changed the public's fascination with these movies.

Not for long, though. A company called Hammer Films, one of the most financially successful film companies in the United Kingdom, soon revived the genre. Founded in 1948 by William Hammer and Sir John Carreras, a former exhibitor, Hammer started out as a distribution company but quickly moved into production. In 1956, Hammer launched a cycle of low-budget horror films that captivated large markets in both England and America. Emphasizing blood and gore in full color, Hammer produced films about Frankenstein, Dracula, the Mummy, and the Wolf Man. With budgets of $500,000 and production schedules that lasted no more than 25 days, the films were heavily promoted and a dozen of them were distributed in America by Universal. The actors most readily identified with the company's horror films are Peter Cushing and Christopher Lee.

Lee played most of the known monsters including Dracula in the 1958 Hammer film. "I stopped appearing as Dracula in 1972," says the actor, "because in my opinion the presentation of the character had deteriorated to such an extent, particularly bringing him into the contemporary day and age, that it really no longer had any meaning."

Peter Cushing also appeared in numerous Hammer horror movies. In the mid-1950s, he became identified with his role as the gaunt, cold-blooded Baron Frankenstein which he played a number of times. He also appeared as Van Helsing in Hammer's 1958 *Dracula*.

The fan base for these classic horror movies greatly increased with the advent of television. In the late 1950s, the networks started using old horror films for programming. Late night shows like *Creature Feature* were hosted by a kitschy celebrity who introduced the Universal black-and-white movies from the 1930s and 1940s to a new generation of kids growing up in the '60s and '70s. Universal Studios Archivist Daryl Maxwell was one of the legions of fans who discovered these movies as a child. "You form strong attachments when you are young," says

LEFT: Early concept drawing of Dracula's bride.

Maxwell, "and these movies worked their magic for all of us who watched them when we were growing up."

Horror films have never totally left the screen; they have just transformed themselves to adjust to the changing taste of the public. "The old horror films hold up," explains screenwriter Curt Siodmak who penned Universal's 1941 *The Wolf Man.* "They were classic tales; the violence was implied, the menace was implied. It wasn't like today, where you cut people open and see blood flying all over the floor. We only had the menace—which was much more tempting and frightening."

More recent horror films have brought the characters into contemporary settings and have certainly spiked the violence. "For the most part, the horror genre has gone the way of the slasher film," explains Daryl Maxwell. "Today it is about body counts and gore. There is no atmosphere, no suspense, no mystery. The most successful recent one, in my opinion, is *Fright Night,* which played with the shared experience so many of us had watching the old films on TV. Roddy McDowell plays a television personality who hosts a show called *Fright Night* that features old horror movies. A kid watches this show, suspects his neighbor is a vampire, and enlists Roddy to help him fight him.

"While the slasher film still has a firm grip on the genre, the last few years have seen some intriguing and hopeful indications that there is an audience that is interested in more than increasingly inventive ways to dispatch someone and the resulting gallons of blood. One trend is to combine elements from two (or more) familiar genres and combine them in interesting ways. In 1998, *Dark City* combined elements of horror, film noir, and science fiction beautifully. And Stephen Sommers' re-imagining of *The Mummy* (1999) and *The Mummy Returns* (2001) successfully combined a classic horror icon with elements taken directly from the serials of the 1930s through 1950s. The productions that seem to work best are the ones that take the well-known conventions and do things that are interesting with them."

A familiar convention within the classic horror genre has always been that the monster never dies. Perhaps the same could be said about horror movies in general. Or, more accurately, perhaps it is true that old monsters never die, they just come back on late night television.

LEFT: Filming a scene with Igor (Kevin J. O'Connor). ABOVE: Poster from Stephen Sommers hit 1999 movie, The Mummy.

Van Helsing: Monster Hunter

The character of Van Helsing, created by Bram Stoker in his 1897 novel, appears in the early Dracula movies. He is the vampire authority; he explains the history of the vampire and points the way for the hero of the story. In the 1930 screenplay written by Tod Browning and Garrett Fort of the first American Dracula movie, even the Count has to admire Van Helsing's intelligence. "For one who has not lived even a single lifetime, you're a wise man, Van Helsing," Dracula concedes.

According to Crash McCreery, the creature designer on Stephen Sommers' *Van Helsing*, the first departure for the character was in the 1958 Hammer film that starred Christopher Lee and Peter Cushing. It was Cushing's idea to add a touch of bravado to the part. "At the end of the film, Peter Cushing was supposed to go over to a window and rip off the curtain, exposing Dracula to the sunlight and killing him. Cushing read the script and said, 'No, it's not enough to just go over and pull the curtain down. I want to run across a twenty-foot-long table and leap fifteen feet through the air to grab onto the curtains.' Instead of just telling someone else what to do, Van Helsing takes charge."

Stephen Sommers expanded greatly on this initial idea. His Van Helsing is a renegade outlaw and a true action hero. "Our Van Helsing is a leading man; he's dynamic and charismatic," says executive producer Sam Mercer. "He is suave. He's a cool character."

Here Van Helsing is a nineteenth-century James Bond and, at heart, he is every man. "He's not superhuman, he's a human who becomes a hero," explains McCreery. "It's not about being born on Krypton or getting bitten by a radioactive spider.

"What I love about a human type of hero is that they become heroes because they don't only hit their pinnacle as far as their capabilities but they surpass it. I think audiences gravitate towards human heroes because they feel that, given the right conditions and in the heat of the moment, they themselves could do the same thing."

LEFT: Hugh Jackman on set in Eastern Europe. ABOVE: Concept drawing for the Hellbeast.

Casting
Creatures

Van Helsing

Hugh Jackman

Director Stephen Sommers had only one actor in mind to play the hero in his movie. "For Van Helsing I needed a guy who was both a man's man and a ladies' man," explains the director. "Women have to love him but men have to trust him. This is hard to pull off; there are a lot of really good-looking actors that women love but men wouldn't trust alone in a room with their wives or girlfriends for five minutes. Hugh, however, is a stand-up guy that women adore and men trust."

Hugh Jackman had just begun filming *X-Men 2* when the director sent him an early draft of the script. "I read the script and loved it," says the actor. "It had an old-fashioned quality that I had not seen since *Raiders of the Lost Ark*. It felt very epic to me but it also had a lightness of touch. I thought the story played with great conviction." Consequently, Jackman agreed to star in the movie.

It was clear that playing Van Helsing would require a great deal of physical work and many stunts, including a lot of wire work. Fortunately, Jackman was in great physical shape by the time he arrived on the *Van Helsing* set. "I was ready," he says. "Although, I have to say that, physically, *Van Helsing* was probably fifty percent tougher than *X-Men*."

In the movie, Jackman plays a classic cinema archetype: the reluctant hero, an outsider on a quest to vanquish evil. But Van Helsing is a complicated character driven by demons he does not understand. "He doesn't know why he is so driven," explains Jackman. "His past is a tormented secret. He is full of conflicts and doesn't understand himself very well. He is not always a nice guy, though ultimately, he is a good guy. He doesn't go by the book but he always gets the job done. He just keeps moving forward. He's that kind of character."

To prepare for the part, the director asked Jackman to watch Errol Flynn movies because Flynn played swashbuckling characters who were very believable. He also asked Jackman to watch *His Girl Friday* and *Casablanca* (because they were old-fashioned romances with lightning-quick dialogue), as well as more recent movies such as *Romancing the Stone* and *Last of the Mohicans*.

By all accounts, Stephen Sommers has a very laid back style of directing, as evidenced in a story that Jackman likes to tell. "On my first day of shooting," Jackman begins, "Steve comes up to me and says, 'This is your first close-up, this is a big movie. Please don't suck.' That was his direction. 'Please don't suck.' He repeated it every day from then on."

Clearly, actor and director share a mutual admiration. "I really believe that the movie could be five hours long and no one would get tired of watching Hugh Jackman," says Sommers. "He's sexy without trying. He's got a lot a mystery to him. And he gets to play with a bunch of really fun weapons."

ANNA VALERIOUS

Kate Beckinsale

"Casting the part of Anna was especially hard," admits Stephen Sommers, "because we had to find an actress who was incredibly beautiful and talented but, considering everything that has happened to her, she had to be a woman, not a girl. Since she's from Transylvania we originally went looking for a European actress. The studio really wanted us to find somebody new. I agreed and we went with that idea. But we soon discovered that it was very hard to find somebody who's a woman, not a girl, incredibly gorgeous and talented but has never done anything. At one point we said, 'We're never going to find this person. Who do we know?' Kate was the first name that came up and that was it."

Producer Bob Ducsay agrees that Anna was the hardest part to cast. "The part required an actress who was extremely strong both as a vampire hunter and as a match for Van Helsing. It was also very important that Anna and Van Helsing have great chemistry, and chemistry is not something you can guarantee." He also agrees that Kate was the perfect actress for the part. "Kate brought a softness to the role which wasn't necessarily in the screenplay but was essential to making the movie work."

In the movie, Beckinsale plays a gypsy princess who is the only survivor of a royal family. "She is not a character who only wears pretty dresses and faints all the time," explains the actress. "She definitely gets her hands dirty and she has a real mission of revenge against Dracula. She's very single-minded which is both her strength and her weakness. She can't really think outside of the box.

"Van Helsing is much more experienced and worldly, and that is one of the reasons why he is so useful to her. He doesn't come at things from such a personal angle. When they meet Frankenstein, for example, she just wants to destroy the monster but Van Helsing sees something else in him and feels sorry for him. As the movie goes along, I think

Anna realizes she was wrong, and that's a big moment because she's not used to admitting she's wrong about anything."

Beckinsale was attracted to the role after reading the script. "It was a nice script with a lot of humor in it," she says, "and I got to dangle on a wire, so I thought it would be good fun."

Ultimately, she got more than she expected. "I did quite a bit of stunt work on *Underworld*," explains the actress. "The difference was that I had three months of training and had worked quite intensely on all of the specific stunts I had to do. Here, I showed up and they said, 'Okay, now you're going to be doing a flip in the forest. Go.' It was much more on the hoof. I had not quite banked on being 40 feet up in the air, dangling upside down in a tree saying to myself, 'I cannot die, I have a small child.'

"One time, I found myself dangling upside down and I was wearing this crucifix as part of my costume. Before I got turned right side up, the crucifix fell out and hit the ground. I thought, 'Oh, God. That's an omen. I'm obviously going to die doing this.' I did have to be talked out of that idea," admits Beckinsale.

Count Dracula
Richard Roxburgh

Although actor Richard Roxburgh, who plays Count Dracula in *Van Helsing*, reread the Bram Stoker book, he got most of his inspiration from wandering the streets of Prague. "The city has a gothic feeling, in abundance," says the actor. "It was kind of easy to feel Dracula-ish in Prague." Roxburgh's extensive theater work in Australia also prepared him for the role. "On stage, you're always called upon to do roles that other people have invented and to reinvent them for yourself. Whether it's Shakespeare or Chekhov, everybody has seen those characters performed and playing Dracula represented the same challenge."

Roxburgh was intrigued by the dual nature of the character. "It has something to do with the quiet torment of a person who has made a compact with the devil," he says. "Dracula will live forever but he is not allowed to feel anything. We can all understand the irony of that situation."

Dracula is also an extremely passionate character. "He is

cursed with an inability to actually feel love," explains Roxburgh. "Yet he has a kind of sense memory of the feeling that I think is similar to an amputee who has phantom pains in a limb that doesn't exist anymore. He has a sense memory of what it was to love and can understand what is missing through a kind of hall of mirrors. That is the emotional fuel where there might otherwise not be one for the character."

Roxburgh admits that he wanted to play with the idea that there was something really alluring about Dracula. "Even though he's very dark, there is a real sexiness to him," he says. "I suppose it's about the way that people are drawn to dark things because they're kind of mysterious and other-worldly and because you don't understand them."

According to Stephen Sommers, the part was written to play up the more modern aspects of the character. "Dracula has been done to death," admits Sommers, "but we put a spin on his character to bring him into this century. We made him like a pompous rock star but in a good way. The movie definitely takes place in the 1880s but somehow Richard was able to make Dracula contemporary. There's something sexy and twisted and really cool about Richard's performance."

CARL

David Wenham

Van Helsing's sidekick, Carl, is a complex character. He is the voice of the audience; he explains and clarifies most of the complex plot lines. In addition, Carl is the film's comic relief; the film often relies upon him to break the tension. In terms of casting, it was crucial to find an actor who could discuss the lore of the werewolf or the legend of Dracula with dead-on believability while, at the same time, be capable of delivering comic lines.

"One day, I got this audition tape and when I played it, I thought the guy's performance was great and he looked perfect for the part," explains Stephen Sommers. "The guy had no neck, these big ears and a terrible haircut. Well, dumb me. Little did I realize that David Wenham is considered one of the sexiest men in Australia. For the audition tape, he gave himself a bad haircut, put black tack behind his ears and hunched himself over so he looked much shorter than Hugh Jackman. I, of course, thought he actually looked like that person on the tape."

Wenham understood, right from the start, that Carl was the audience's eyes and ears. "Van Helsing and Anna have been out hunting Dracula in this world for quite some time," says Wenham. "Carl hasn't, so it's a new experience for him; he's open, he's objective, and he is genuinely scared and frightened, just like the audience.

"Carl is a funny little character who has spent most of his life in a strange place underneath the Vatican in Rome. He has never really been outside. 'Earnest' is the adjective that Stephen used to use to best sum him up.

"Carl invents the most extraordinary weapons but never goes out and uses them. When he meets Van Helsing, he's forced to go on an adventure. In the end, he is a better person for the experience.

"Carl is an extremely intelligent, creative, and inventive character who thinks laterally," explains Wenham. "So he's a good foil for Van Helsing who is the physical brute force,

strength, and charisma of the piece. The two of them trust each other completely. Van Helsing certainly needs Carl's intelligence to get them through problems that occur throughout the film. Ultimately, Carl realizes that he is part of the Van Helsing mission to vanquish evil from the world."

Working so closely with Hugh Jackman became a personal challenge for Wenham. "Hugh has a reputation for being one of the nicest people in show business. I came onto this shoot with the mission to find something about Hugh to debunk that theory," jokes Wenham. "So far, I've failed. Hugh is genuinely the most generous, happy, and uplifting person. However, I still believe there has got to be something bad about him. I intend to find it eventually and go on *E!* with an exclusive."

ÍGOR

Kevin J. O'Connor

Kevin J. O'Connor worked on Stephen Sommer's *The Mummy* and during the shoot, the director mentioned the idea of having the actor play Igor. "Stephen said to me that he thought the part of Igor would be great for me," explains the actor. "It was so funny. I had not thought of that for years and years. Then they sent me the script for *Van Helsing* and offered me the role of Igor. It hit me that Stephen had mentioned that before. So it came full circle around."

To re-create the character of Igor—who is surely as familiar to audiences as Frankenstein or Count Dracula—O'Connor was inspired by magazines such as *Eerie* and *Creepy* which often featured full-color paintings of Igor and other creatures. "The covers were always beautiful," says O'Connor. "And, at first, Igor was more like a drawing to me than a character. I went and looked at those covers and they propelled me into the character."

Another inspiration was Lon Chaney Sr., the star of many silent movies. "I always loved what Chaney did with his body," explains the actor. "I am not saying that I compare myself to him but he did inspire me."

O'Connor spent a long time perfecting Igor's walk. His first idea was that Igor could barely move but then he realized that there were scenes where the character was running so the actor had to compromise the concept. In the end, he found the perfect looping gait for the character.

Another major inspiration for the actor was his makeup. "I had some early indication that the makeup was going to be pretty extensive," says O'Connor. "At first, the process of getting into makeup took about five hours but then we got it down to about four hours. I had to get to the set hours before anyone else when it was just the two makeup guys, a security guard, and me. There were days when, by the time I finally got to the set, I felt like I'd worked a full day already. Wearing the makeup was not as bad as I thought it would be. It was hot and itchy but it wasn't that uncomfortable and it

was exciting to have it on and start to play with it."

O'Connor created an interesting back story for his character. "Igor is a grave robber," explains the actor. "He's been beaten up, thrown off carts, run over, and kicked by a mule. He has been around monsters and corpses and things for a long time.

"Igor betrays Dr. Frankenstein by going off with Count Dracula and letting the doctor die. He understands the power of Dracula, but he's also been such a sycophant, he's mastered the art of kissing butt from Dr. Frankenstein. Igor understands how to survive. Besides, working for the Count is a better job opportunity and he's going up the corporate ladder. Pays a little better. Maybe he gets better benefits. He's so happy to have work and be fed. And he has no choice, so he makes the best of it."

FRANKENSTEIN'S MONSTER

Shuler Hensley

During production, Tony Award-winner Shuler Hensley spent more than four hours in make-up every day watching himself being transformed into Frankenstein's monster. He wore dentures and a costume that weighed almost fifty pounds. The only benefit to his heavy costume was that it kept him warm in the chilly Prague weather. His costume, he says, functioned as thermal underwear.

Fiberglass tubes were molded to his feet in a slightly pointed position so that the six-foot, three-inch tall actor actually appeared to tower over seven feet. The stilts made walking somewhat difficult but gave Hensley an awkward gait that worked for the part he was playing.

The movie opens with a classic horror-movie scene of an angry mob of villagers screaming for the blood of the monster. "I've done nothing wrong and yet you all want to see me dead," Frankenstein's Monster says in the screenplay. This line was key to the character for Hensley. "I think it is easy to relate to him at that point," the actor says. "Everyone has felt like an outsider at some time in their life."

But the shock value of the monster's appearance goes away once his character is revealed. "I think the monster is really only looking for love and acceptance," Hensley explains. "He discovers that Dracula wants to use him to make a super-race of vampires and that, if he's ever captured, it would be the end of everyone. So he's caught in this dilemma but, in the end, he'd rather die than serve Dracula. I think we can all relate to his good side and, ultimately, you wind up pulling for him."

Although Shuler Hensley had not done much movie work previous to *Van Helsing*, he knew Hugh Jackman from his theater work. The two appeared together on the London stage in a much-acclaimed production of *Oklahoma*. "Hugh is like my little brother," says Hensley. "Right after *Oklahoma*, Hugh went off to make the first *X-Men*. I went back to New York and I worked with him on *Someone Like You*.

When I had my *Van Helsing* audition, I had no idea who else was cast. I asked who was in the movie and they said, 'A guy named Hugh Jackman.'"

The two actors enjoyed working together and, between takes, often broke into songs from *Oklahoma*. In costume, they both sang "Happy Birthday" to the director.

Hensley's little girl, Schuyler, was a frequent visitor to the set and often spent her afternoons playing with Kate Beckinsale's young daughter. "All the kids on the set loved Frankenstein's monster," says Hensley. "The first time my daughter saw me in costume, she acted a bit strange until I started speaking to her in 'Daddy's' voice. Then she thought it was the funniest thing. Actually, I think my child prefers 'Daddy-monster' to 'Daddy.' I'm sure that'll mean years of therapy for her in later life."

VELKAN VALERIOUS
Will Kemp

From the very beginning, the filmmakers wanted their Wolf Man to be completely different from anything anyone had seen before. "I watched the original, Universal *Wolf Man* and I realized that this guy was really a tormented soul," says Stephen Sommers. "He wanted to be good but he just couldn't help himself. I felt a lot of sympathy and empathy for the character."

The actor Will Kemp auditioned for the part in London and was one of the first actors that the filmmakers interviewed. "Even though he hadn't done anything before, his audition was just spectacular," says Sommers. "There was real power to his performance."

Kemp is a dancer, and he was able to use his body for the transformation into the Wolf Man that was nothing short of spectacular. "We wanted him right away but because we had not yet cast the leading lady, who was his sister, we couldn't hire him yet. We had to hire the leading lady before we hired her brother," explains Sommers. "So we kept Will on the hook for months while we searched for our leading lady. Eventually it all worked out. The funny thing was nobody knew who he was until I mentioned that he was that guy in the Gap commercial. Then people, especially the women, would say, 'Oh, that guy!?'"

Verona

Marishka

Aleera

THE BRIDES

ALEERA Elena Anaya
VERONA Silvia Colloca
MARISHKA Josie Maran

Stephen Sommers wrote three brides of Dracula into his screenplay and then discovered that casting the parts was a long and difficult process. The filmmakers looked at many, many actresses.

Bob Ducsay got an audition tape of Elena Anaya, an actress he had seen in *Sex and Lucia*, and he recommended her to Sommers. "I looked at the audition tape and thought she was gorgeous, sexy, and totally insane," says the director. "She was perfect for Aleera. But then I figured I'd better meet her. What if this tape was only a record of her personality? What if she wasn't an actress but just a nut ball?"

In London, Sommers met Elena and soon discovered that she was very sweet, very quiet, and not at all insane. She had, indeed, been acting on her tape. "She came in and just knocked it out of the ballpark," says Sommers.

That same day, Priscilla John, the casting director in London, told Sommers that she'd found an Italian actress who would be perfect for the part of Verona. "Silvia Colloca was not only physically right for the part but she spoke English with an Italian accent that was just off a little bit," says Sommers. "That was exactly how I imagined Verona speaking."

Finding two of the brides was a coup. Soon after returning to the United States, Sommers met with Josie Maran, a model, and hired her immediately.

The three actresses bonded immediately and each brought a different energy to their roles that was completely distinctive. The women enjoyed working together, even though they would soon discover that their job included some serious stunt work. They would spend weeks hanging upside down or performing other strenuous tasks on a blue screen stage. Encased in rigging, the girls were swept across the set. They were constantly being twisted and turned into impossible positions.

Though all three actresses were in top athletic shape, the physical strain of performing as the brides was enormous. "By the end of the shoot, those girls were limping and I don't think they'll have to do any more abdominal work for the next few years," says Sommers. "After this film, I told them that they should double their fees whenever they have to work on a blue screen stage. If they have to wear contact lenses and spend eight hours a day having a guy blast hot wind in their faces, they should triple their fees."

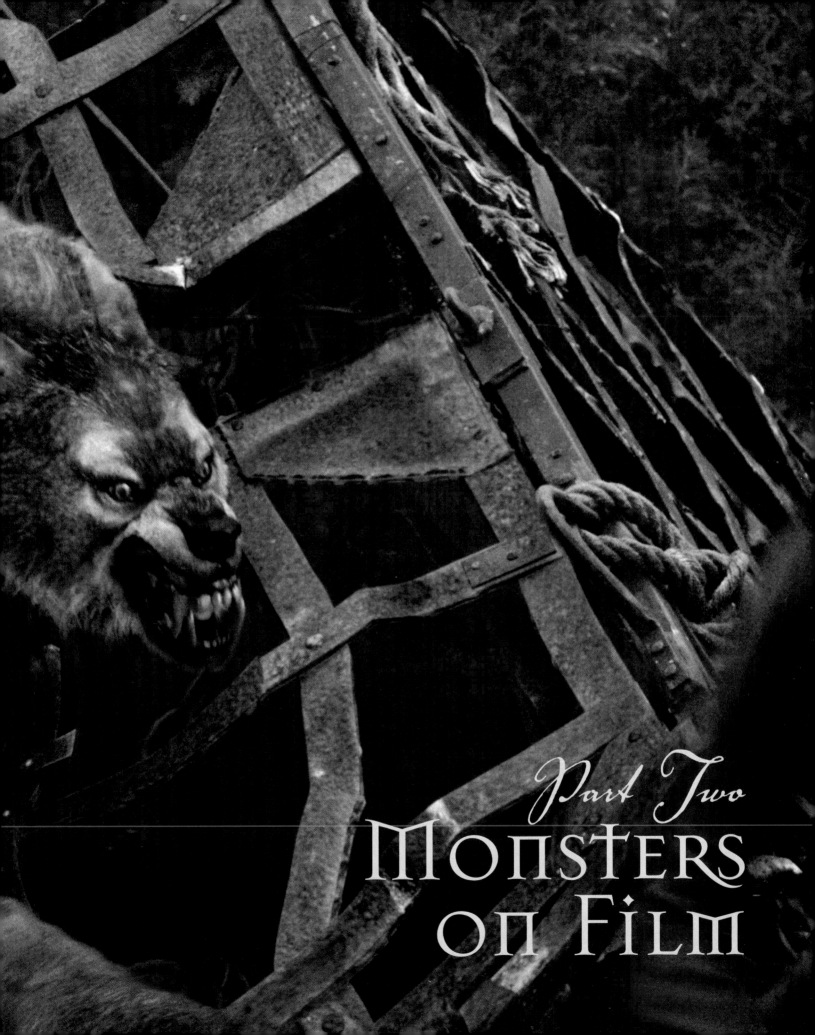

Part Two

Monsters on Film

Castles & Candlelight: Production Design

"The movie takes place in the late 1880s, which is a great period for me to design," says production designer Allan Cameron who has collaborated on three movies with Stephen Sommers. "I love the late Victorian period. It's a make-believe world and we are in Transylvania for a lot of it."

The first order of business was to find a location. Cameron immediately thought of Eastern Europe. "This is the fourth film that I've done in the Czech Republic," he says, "so I know quite a lot of the castles and which ones have the right atmosphere and look for the movie. I took photographs of the landscapes, towns, and castles to Los Angeles to show Stephen, and he liked the feel of the country. We both came to the Czech Republic to scout, and we found most of the locations we needed."

It was decided that half the movie would be filmed in the Czech Republic and the other half would be shot on a stage in Los Angeles. "We broke it down so that Prague focused on the look of the picture, taking advantage of the architecture, and Los Angeles was more about telling the story," explains executive producer Sam Mercer.

Prague is a well-established country for making films and has a very fine facility with experienced technicians. "You can source a lot of stuff in the city although, like anywhere, there are certain things that you can't find," says art director Giles Masters. "Many of the props and set decorations for *Van Helsing* were shipped in from other countries. Even so, we were very happy with all the construction done in Prague. Their machine shop and their metal shop were superb."

Prague was also selected because of the weather. "They guaranteed us gray skies," says Mercer. "We ended up with two weeks of sun, which really played havoc with our schedule." Directors don't usually complain about sunny skies but, as Sommers says, "Vampires can't live in the sun, and we had too much sun."

Many of the skies were altered in post-production to make them more roiling and scary and, of course, to remove all of the rigs and, in the end, the weather in Prague had many benefits. "Because it was winter when we shot there, we got a lot of mileage out of the cold weather," adds producer Bob Ducsay. "The people in the movie

I TRY TO WORK WITH ONLY THE BEST OF THE BEST, SO THEY ALL MAKE ME LOOK GOOD.

—STEPHEN SOMMERS

BELOW: *Producer/editor Bob Ducsay and production designer Allan Cameron during production.*

The Atmosphere

"One of the wonderful things that Stephen has done to anchor the audience in this world was to shoot the opening sequence in black and white," says executive producer, Sam Mercer. "It really sets the tone for Frankenstein's world."

inhabit a very dark, difficult world and when they speak, we can see breath coming out of their mouths."

As for the sets, Stephen Sommers insisted that they be absolutely believable. "The audience needed to believe that everything was real," explains the director, "so we could not be flying a camera around a miniature model set. I wanted to build an entire village and fly a camera around that, and that became quite a task."

Working from his studio in England, Cameron and his team of artists sketched the sets, created architectural drawings of the structures, and then turned the drawings into working models. Once approved in Los Angeles, the drawings and models were transferred to the Czech Republic, where they were constructed by a team of plasterers, carpenters, and metal workers. After the sets were built, set decorator Anna Pinnock added the finishing details. The whole process of designing the sets took about six months.

"The design of the Transylvania village was slightly hyper-real," explains Ducsay. "The roofs were canted and the place had a Dr. Caligari-type feel to it. But at the same time, on film it looked very realistic. Cinematographer Allen Daviau was very particular about the amount of smoke he used, which gave it a realism within sort of a hyper-real environment, exactly what we wanted for the design of the movie."

"The village that they built just outside Prague was really spectacular and will be standing longer than many of the castles in Prague," says Hugh Jackman. "The only problem for us was that the ground was dirt. There was no pavement or cobblestones, just a layer of straw. Of course, the snow came and then the rain and by the time we were shooting with about a thousand extras there all day, the mud was up to your ankles. I think the Czech people enjoyed seeing all these L.A. people trudging through the mud in their Prada snow boots."

Dracula's Castle

The set for Dracula's Castle was enormous, measuring 300 feet long, 120 feet wide, and 60 feet high. The castle was constructed with a modern kind of foam, using the same technique as plaster. Although foam is more expensive than plaster, it dries quicker, is much lighter to use, and requires less material and manpower.

The foundation of the castle was painted black to reflect the lights and give the set a more dramatic feel. "The overall look of the castle was meant to be dark, gothic, and very mysterious," adds production designer Allan Cameron.

"We spent about twelve weeks actually building the castle," says Cameron. "We shot there for four days and, in the end, it will probably be about five or six minutes of finished film. So it's a long process to get five or six minutes of film."

The countryside of the Czech Republic was used for exterior shots of Transylvania in winter in such scenes as the coach chase.

ABOVE: *The Transylvania set was appropriately eerie.* LEFT: *Cinematographer Allen Daviau.* RIGHT: *An early concept model of the Transylvania set that was constructed in pre-production.*

Iconic Images

Dracula's castle is only one of many iconic references in the movie. "What makes Stephen a terrific director is his lack of cynicism," says producer Bob Ducsay. "He believes in this world. He approaches these movies with an open heart. I think the joy you feel in his movies comes from his belief and his joy in making them."

LEFT: Realized shot of Castle Dracula. RIGHT: Concept drawing of Castle Dracula. ABOVE: Set model of the entrance to the castle and a still from the actual set as it appears in the film.

Production Design

Masquerade Ball

St. Nicholas, the premier Baroque church in the Czech Republic, was one of the first places that the director and production designer scouted. The church is deconsecrated and used for concerts and other events. Obtaining permission to shoot in this amazing, historical structure involved a great deal of intense negotiation by the location managers.

Although the filmmakers were able to obtain permission, it came with many restrictions. No wire rigging was allowed in the church, so a duplicate set was created at another location to shoot the flying and trapeze work. Worst of all, at least for the actors, the filmmakers were not allowed to heat the interior space, even though they were shooting in the middle of the winter. Despite the restrictions, the filmmakers were anxious to use the church because constructing a set from scratch with all the features of the church would have cost a fortune.

The masquerade ball represents one of the premiere moments in the film and involved the participation of almost every department. Wardrobe, makeup and hair, visual effects, and the camera and art departments were all pressed into service to set this scene. Hundreds of extras had to be costumed by Gabriella Pescucci. "It's the *pièce de resistance* in the film," explains art director Giles Masters, "and a chance for everybody to really express themselves and to have fun."

The actual preparation of the church took about a month. First, anything ecclesiastical was either removed or hidden. All the pews were removed and the rough concrete floor was covered with a dance floor. The drape and prop department used fabric and Baroque-style screens to cover the confessionals and any statues holding crosses. Candelabras and mirrors were brought into the set.

The ambiance of the ball called for massive amounts of candlelight but real candles burn quickly and can cause both smoke and fire. Instead of actual candles, the prop department constructed oil-burning lamps that looked like candles but gave off almost no heat or smoke. The lamps could burn for more than eight hours at a time. "We can't hold up the film to light 150 candles," explains Masters. "We would need an entire team just on candle watch. Our job is to keep things moving. We never want the camera waiting for us."

Once the set was decorated it was turned over to the choreographer so that she and her 150 dancers could rehearse in the actual location where they would be filming. Because this was Dracula's ball, the dancing sequence would have to be something out of the ordinary.

"It takes me about ten seconds to get bored with a dancing scene, especially late nineteenth-century dancing," says Sommers.

DRACULA PUTS ON A
HELL OF A BALL AT
ST. NICHOLAS CHURCH.
HE'S A VERY DECADENT
AND EXCITING GUY WHO
CERTAINLY KNOWS HOW
TO THROW A PARTY. IN
HOLLYWOOD, HE WOULD
DEFINITELY FIT IN.

—BOB DUCSAY, PRODUCER/EDITOR

51

"So what we wanted to shoot was the most insane, spectacular costume ball anyone had ever seen, and it had to be fairly twisted as this was Dracula's masquerade ball. I asked for flamethrowers and jugglers and high-wire acts. I wanted a veritable Cirque de Soleil."

Debra Brown, who has choreographed numerous Cirque de Soleil shows, was hired to work on the ballroom sequence. For the elaborate dance scene, she used 100 trained ballroom dancers from Prague, seventeen local circus artists, four circus artists from other parts of the world, artists from the Cirque de Soleil, and a variety of contortionists, gymnasts, flying trapeze artists, and jugglers. "It was a huge collaboration that involved many different artists and two different languages," explains Brown.

All of the preparation was well worth the effort for this amazing set, which proved inspirational for the actors. "It's extraordinary to bring this visitation of pure evil into a Baroque cathedral," says Richard Roxburgh. "Whether or not the church is deconsecrated, it still has the feeling of a place of worship. Slightly twisted, of course, in this sense."

Kate Beckinsale was equally impressed, though she adds that the church itself "was, I think, the coldest place I've ever been in my life. It was freezing in Prague but it was colder inside that church than it was outdoors, maybe because the church was built of stone. I was surprised that we didn't all come out looking blue on screen."

While the church itself was used in long shots, many of the close-ups, especially those involving special effects, were shot on a set in Los Angeles that was created to exactly replicate certain areas of St. Nicholas.

After shooting in the church was completed, the crew spent two weeks returning the space to its original incarnation. Today, the church appears exactly as it was before the cast and crew descended on it. No one would ever suspect that this imperial space was ever used for a masked ball thrown by none other than Count Dracula himself.

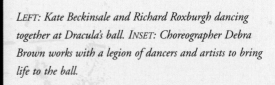

LEFT: Kate Beckinsale and Richard Roxburgh dancing together at Dracula's ball. INSET: Choreographer Debra Brown works with a legion of dancers and artists to bring life to the ball.

53

The locations for *Van Helsing*, both real and imagined, were nothing short of spectacular. Sometimes the real places were as amazing as those that were created for the movie. These original concepts for matte painting were designed by Illusion Arts and include shots of Vatican City (top), St. Peters (above) Notre Dame (above left), The Eiffel Tower (far left), Budapest (below left), and Valerious Mansion (center).

CREATURE CREATION

> A THERAPIST WOULD
> HAVE A FIELD DAY
> ON THIS FILM.
>
> —HUGH JACKMAN

Like many movie fans, Crash McCreery has had a life-long fascination with horror movies. "For me, it started with *King Kong*, my earliest memory of any kind of monster film," he recalls. "I remember staying up till midnight with my best friend to see what was on *Creature Feature*. Something about characters from other worlds and the fantasy element really sparked my imagination. Ever since then, I've been fascinated with animals or characters that didn't actually exist." Not everyone, however, gets to spend their career bringing these characters to life, which was McCreery's job as the creature designer on *Van Helsing*.

Early in production, McCreery was approached by producer Bob Ducsay and brought on board to help create the monsters in the movie. "It is every designer's dream to work on werewolves and vampires," McCreery says. "I was also really attracted to the idea that Stephen wanted to make it a period movie. Today it seems that most people want to create alternative or futuristic stories with these Gothic creatures."

From the very start, McCreery was conscious of the huge fan base for these characters and of not upsetting those fans with designs that were too far off-base or radically different from the original creations. "Stephen is such a huge fan of those original characters that he was always conscious of retaining the original mythology while still wanting to show the audience something different and exciting," McCreery explains.

Creating a believable monster, for McCreery, means looking deep into the character and capturing the human side of its essence. "The most successful monsters that have been caught on film are the ones that have the kind of motivation that speaks to humans in a very primordial and base way," explains the designer. "They are all struggling with some eternal, internal emotion or desire or drive."

ABOVE: Creature designer Crash McCreery at the drawing table.

The Hellbeast

McCreery began his work on the Hellbeast by taking the nightmarish image of what Dracula represented and bringing that to life. "The designs didn't have much to do with the actor or a human," he says. "It was more about the representation of Dracula's essence of evil and using elements of that essence that would kind of creep us out."

Bats are very prevalent in vampire features so the designer began with basic characteristics. "We enhanced that with giant claws and pumped him full of adrenaline to make this super, über-bat creature that is terrifying and powerful," he explains.

ABOVE: Six-step concept drawing of Dracula's transformation into the Hellbeast. RIGHT: Concept drawing of the Hellbeast LEFT: Facial expresion drawings for the Hellbeast and still of the Hellbeast from the film. OPPOSITE PAGE: Concept drawing of the Hellbeast.

The Werewolves

To create a character like The Wolf Man, the artists began by looking at nature. Even though the character was a creature of fantasy, it had to be grounded in reality. So the team analyzed the cast of a real wolf skull, studying such anatomical elements as the teeth and jaw structure. "It's a fine line between getting too real and creating a new, cool, kind of fresh animal," says ILM art director Christian Alzmann. The character was computer-generated (CG) so sketches made by the *Van Helsing* artists were sent to ILM to create the monster.

"A single shot for any of the synthetic characters such as the werewolves will take months and months of work by 50 or 60 people to produce," says visual effects associate producer Joe Grossberg. "No matter how good the animators are or how specific the direction, it's a slow, slow process. The movie wrapped in July and we worked on the synthetic characters right up until the time the movie released in May of the following year."

Various designs for the look of Frankenstein's Monster. The artists worked to combine elements of the original character with a fresh and distinctive look.

Frankenstein's Monster

When the filmmakers were designing the look of Frankenstein's Monster, they began with the original creature. "I wanted to keep certain elements of his look: the flat-top head, the bolts, and the Doc Martens on his feet," says Stephen Sommers. "Then we wanted to enhance the look, to make it cooler and different. We made a change to the back of his head where we added a piece of glass. We get to see an electrical storm inside his brain. When he's calm, it's just little flickers of lightning inside his head but when he's angry, the electricity goes wild."

"Being able to see through the glass piece was our new take on Frankenstein's Monster," says creature concept artist Patrick Tatopoulos. "Without looking robotic, the device was somewhere between a steam machine and a human being." According to makeup artist Greg Cannom, sculpting and designing the Frankenstein monster was one of the most fascinating challenges in the movie. "We had a lot of fun working on Frankenstein," he says. "Stephen really wanted him to have a real humanity and to be designed so that the actor's face would show through."

Here is a Frankenstein monster that melds the best of the past with a fresh, modern take. Creature designer Crash McCreery began by exploring some basic questions: Can the body twist? Is it mechanical? How much is organic and how much of him is man-made? He also stayed focused on the monster's personality and his innate embarrassment about his looks. "In some of the costume designs we played with him trying to hide his face and his identity," says McCreery. "Part of his character is his consciousness of his displacement in the world. Frankenstein's Monster was created against his will and in a very unnatural way. He is supposed to be a human being, but he looks nothing like a human, and has never had a birthing experience or a growing-up experience. Imagine being thirty-four years old and suddenly brought into this world without ever having learned anything as a child. Add to that, that you look incredibly grotesque. To me, the character of Frankenstein's Monster has always been about dealing with the human emotion of trying to fit in and trying to make sense of your existence."

The Dwergi

In terms of the story, director Stephen Sommers felt that Igor needed some helpers and that was the inspiration for the characters known as the Dwergi in the movie. "I didn't want them to be CG creatures," says Sommers. "I've got enough CG things going on. Then I realized that they didn't have to be CG. I gave them a reason to be com-

pletely covered from head to foot: they're always welding, soldering and hammering so they have to wear armor and goggles. After that, the designers came up with the look to go with the characters."

Creature designer Crash McCreery, conceived of the idea that the Dwergi were experiments gone wrong. "I imagined that they needed some apparatus to survive for breathing or seeing which was hidden beneath their cloaks," he says. "Dracula kept them around as his minions because they could go out and fetch body parts or whatever other task had to be done."

The look that McCreery designed wasn't so much to create a character but more to hide what was inside it. "I think it's more interesting to cover something up and leave the audience wondering," he explains. "It also gave them a kind of 'Industrial Revolution' feel that permeates the design of the movie."

ABOVE: Concept drawings of a Dwerger mask.
ABOVE CENTER: The final mask seen in the movie.
RIGHT: Concept drawing for the Dwergi. BACK-
GROUND: The Dwergi at work during filming.

Pygmy Bat Pods

We talked a lot about the pods, what their layering might look like and how these things are suspended in a cocoon," says creature designer Crash McCreery. "My original idea was that it was like a beehive full of these pods. There was a lot of exploration about how much the offspring inside the egg can be seen."

ABOVE: Two early concept drawings for the Baby Bat Pods. BACKGROUND: Actors on the set in the egg room chamber.

Pygmy Bats

"The Pygmy bats were supposed to be the spawn of Dracula and his brides, but Stephen said they didn't have to look like them," says Christian Alzmann, ILM art director. "He only wanted the bats to look nasty, so we made them so ugly that you want to kick them. The audience will be relieved when they die. The eyes in these creatures are especially important to convey anger and a menacing threat."

LEFT: Concept drawings of Pygmy bats. ABOVE: Pygmy bat model. TOP: Realized Pygmy bat in the film.

68

The Brides

While ILM faced many unique challenges in bringing Dracula and The Wolf Man to life, nothing had quite prepared them for the daunting task of transforming three beautiful actresses into Dracula's hellish brides. "Stephen didn't want computer-graphic faces for the brides," explains ILM visual effects supervisor Scott Squires. "He wanted them to be flying around close to the camera and to respond to actors." This required complex visual effects technology—a marriage of flesh and fiction that had never before been accomplished on this scale. "We decided to shoot the actresses and then merge their faces with CG bodies," explains Squires, whose "hybrid" tests proved to filmmakers that it was possible for a digital creature to retain the face—and thus the performance—of an actress.

Silvia Colloca, Elena Anaya, and Josie Maran's first chance to sink their teeth into the roles of Dracula's brides came on the set of the Transylvanian village. While they performed the more "human" aspects of their characters for the cameras, ILM began the process that would turn them into some of the movie's most memorable monsters. Charting the flight paths of Dracula's spouses with complex cable-cam rigs, the visual effects supervisors then photographed the actresses in full creature makeup against a blue screen in Los Angeles—more than half a world away from where their work on the scene first began. These performances provided the body movements and facial expressions audiences see as the brides rocket through the village.

On screen, what the audience will finally see is what ILM calls a "Hybrid Bride"; she is part human and part computer graphic. She flies across the screen on her computer-generated wings but, as the camera pans her face, it is the actress that the audience will see.

I think it is every actress's dream to play a vampire.

—Silvia Colloca, Verona

Opposite, above, and right: Early concept drawings of a vampire bride. Far right: Elena Anaya as Aleera. Below: Concept sketches of Verona's transformation.

71

According to makeup artist Greg Cannom, the brides wore two different sets of makeup; one for when they were supposed to look beautiful and the other for their horror shots. "The brides were monsters, of course," explains ILM art director Christian Alzmann, "but they were also sexy, attractive women and their look needed to incorporate both sides of their personality." In the end, the beauty makeup for the brides took about forty minutes to apply, and the horror makeup, which included various prosthetics, about twice as long. "My favorite part was the ears," says Elena Anaya (Aleera).

ABOVE: Aleera (Elena Anaya) with prosthetic fangs and contact lenses. LEFT: Concept drawing of the Brides. OPPOSITE: Marishka (Josie Maran), top, and Verona (Silvia Colloca) at their vampire best.

Monster Makeup

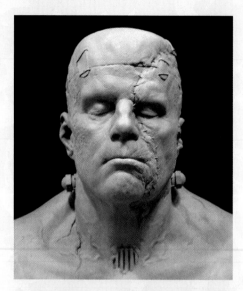

Creating the makeup for the monsters in *Van Helsing* was an enormous challenge for Academy Award-winning makeup artist Greg Cannom. Most of the characters in the movie, especially Frankenstein, were already well-known icons and had appeared in many previous movies. "It's very scary at first," says Cannom, "because you want to create something that has not been seen before. Also, when you are creating makeups like this, you are constantly battling how far to go. You don't want to lose the actor under all that makeup."

The work on Frankenstein's Monster was perhaps the most complex of any of the creatures in the movie. "Shuler has such a great face," explains Cannom, "that we really wanted to see it through the makeup. We wanted a real humanity to the character." The problem was to find the balance between the actor and his makeup.

"When I first started thinking about Frankenstein's Monster, I wanted the Nautilus look of an old ship, all old iron, rivets, and black rust. Then we thought it would be cool if we split the head open and put big cracks in it. But Stephen didn't want it to be too gory. You start out with these simple ideas and then take it from there."

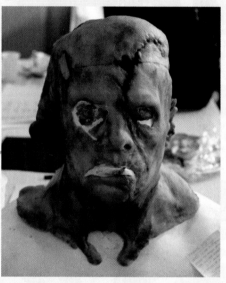

The process began with casting the actor's face. Cannom flew to New York where Shuler Hensley, the actor cast as Frankenstein's Monster, was starring in *Oklahoma* on Broadway (for which he won a Tony). Between performances, the actor was fitted for a head cast. Back in Los Angeles, Cannom and sculptor Glenn Hans designed the look of the monster by adding elements to the actor's head cast. Makeup was created from silicone which is much lighter and more translucent than foam or rubber. The makeup added bulk and other elements to the face including metal pieces. Copper teeth were created, as were special contact lenses.

Finding the right coloring for the makeup was another big challenge. The monster appears in black and white in the beginning of the film and, although the rest of the film is shot in color, Cannom wanted him to carry through as though he was still monochromatic. "I didn't want a lot of flesh colors on the neck," says Cannom. "In the beginning, we tried making him green but that looked really awful. We settled on a grayish color that took weeks and weeks to perfect. Getting the right color was very difficult but we got it to work so that he still had kind of a black-and-white look to him that I really liked."

The artists then began the process of creating a body suit that would completely re-sculpt the actor's body and fit a frame that would make him about seven feet tall. His waist was lengthened, his shoulders were built-up and his head was expanded. His arms and fingers were lengthened

ABOVE: A cast of Shuler Hensley's head was made for the artists to create his makeup. Silicone was then added to the original cast to reshape the head and add elements such as scars. BELOW and RIGHT: Hensley in full makeup.

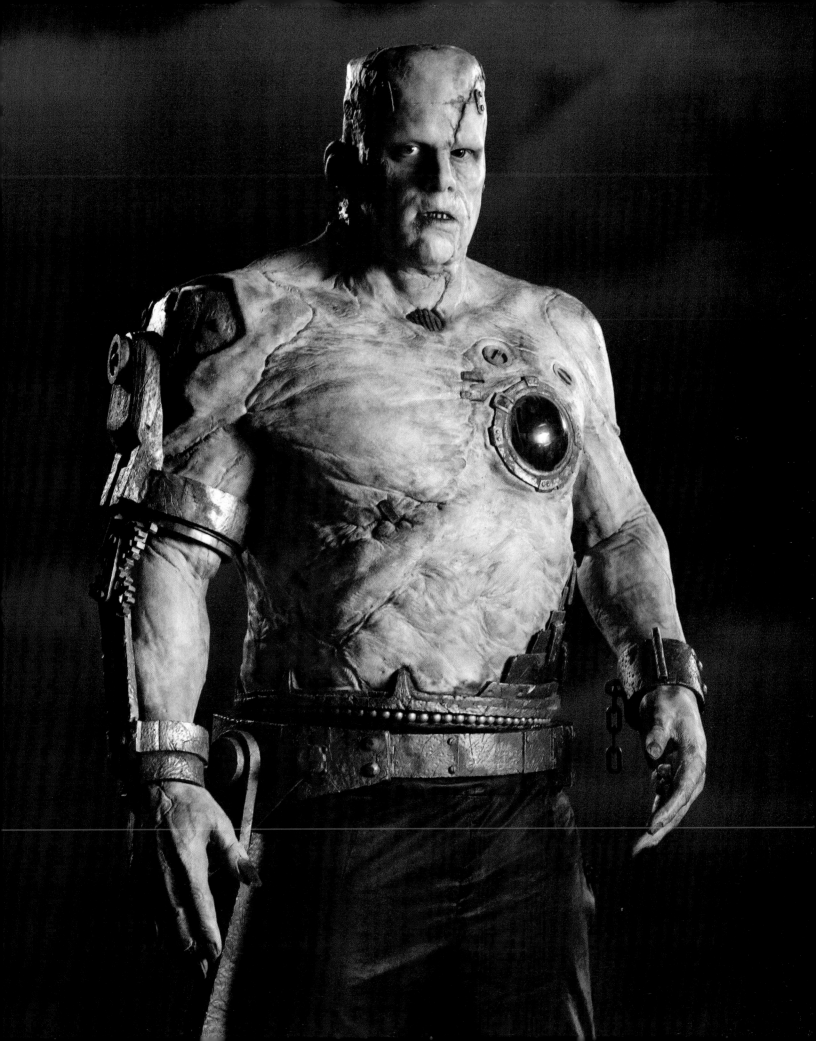

LEFT: Details from the back of Frankenstein's Monster showing his extensive scars. ABOVE: CGI effect of the head of Frankenstein's Monster split open. BELOW: On set Shuler Hensley was surrounded by a team of technicians.

to such a degree that they required mechanical fittings to make them movable.

"We built these huge fingers," says Cannom, "and then I thought it would be cool to add big copper fingernails that looked like they had been stitched on randomly. It was amazing how the hands really completed the look. Unfortunately, the hands were hard for the actor to wear because they were so huge that he couldn't pick things up with them."

In the end, the most important part was making Frankenstein's Monster look human so that the audience would believe he was a real person and have compassion for him. "I was really happy that Stephen wanted him done in makeup and not as a computer-generated character. The only CGI element is the lightning storm in the brain but, other than that, the whole thing was done in makeup," says Cannom.

Getting an actor into his makeup is always a long and tedious process but creating a Frankenstein's Monster makes the work even more complicated. The first time that Shuler Hensley was made up, the process took seven hours. Eventually, the crew got the routine down to five hours. Two makeup artists worked for about three and a half hours and then it took another three people an hour and a half

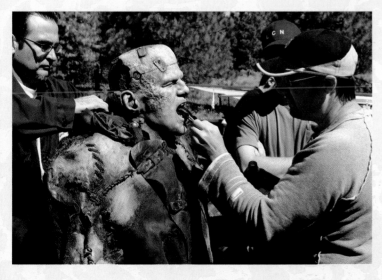

to get the actor into his body suit. Other people were on hand to handle the mechanics of the hands and other elements of his look such as his contact lens and teeth. "So, when he walks on set, there's about seven or eight people following him," says Cannom.

"I felt like Britney Spears with my eight or nine handlers," Hensley jokes.

"This is one of the hardest makeup jobs I have ever done," Cannom adds. "Every day we're creating Frankenstein's Monster from scratch. The first time is so exciting, but about three weeks into it, you're thinking 'Oh, God, not again.'"

DRESSED TO KILL: COSTUMES

Gabriella Pescucci is an Academy Award-winning costume designer with almost forty movies to her credit including such period pieces as *The Age of Innocence* and *Cousin Bette*. The Italian designer was vacationing on a beach in Tunisia when she got a call from Stephen Sommers asking her to work on *Van Helsing*. Within a few weeks, she was in Los Angeles sketching designs.

"I did a lot of research," says Pescucci, "because this movie is both a period piece set in the late 1880s and a fantasy film." The designer's challenge was to meld these two aspects of the movie into workable, wearable costumes.

For the title character, Pescucci was asked to create not only a costume but a recognizable image. "My major concern with Van Helsing's costume," says Stephen Sommers, "was that, even if he were silhouetted against the moon and only in profile, even if you could not see his face, the audience should always know it was him. That was all I said to Gabriella; she took it from there."

The recognizable silhouette would of course include a hat, an accessory that Jackman knew would cause problems. "When I got the script, it included a pencil drawing of Van Helsing," explains the actor. "He had a mask up to his nose and the iconic hat. The problem was I have the kind of head that hats just hate. I've never looked good in a hat. I've been in several movies where I was supposed to wear a hat but, in the end, the hat got tossed out the window. I don't know, small head on a big body or something, it just doesn't work.

"Steve assured me that Gabriella would find a hat that worked for

ABOVE: Costume designer Gabriella Pescucci adjusts the costume for Hugh Jackman while filming on location. RIGHT: Some of the many, many original designs for the Van Helsing character.

me, but after trying about five different styles, she said, 'He can't wear a hat. There's no hat that fits him.' In the end, I wound up with one larger hat for the long shots and a smaller one for the close-ups. The hat for the long shots is huge; up close it makes me look like I am child wearing my father's hat."

Kate Beckinsale's wardrobe combined elements of both period costumes and a more modern look. "Anna, the princess, wears trousers during the day when she is with Van Helsing," says Pescucci. "At night, she wears dresses. She is a sexy, strong woman and we made a beautiful red dress for her ballroom scene. These are the two faces of Anna."

Beckinsale, the star of more than one action movie, had her own problems with the costumes. "The costumes looked fantastic but they were not entirely practical," she admits. "I had to do a lot of running around in rather high, spindly heels and tight corsets. I had to swim in a massive ball gown. I always think if a woman gets through an action movie, she's way tougher than the guys because they usually get to wear sneakers and pants."

Pescucci spent many hours sketching the costume for Count Dracula. Her first idea was to give him a contemporary look. "But Stephen didn't want him to look like a pop star," she says. "So then we decided to use an eighteenth-century style with a modern touch mixed in."

Costume design for the movie also involved creating wardrobes for hundreds of extras. More than 400 villagers in the opening scene and 350 dancers in the masquerade ball needed to be costumed. Many of the clothes were stitched in Rome and then sent to Prague where much of the intricate embroidery work was done by native seamstresses in the Czech Republic. The costumes worn during the masquerade ball are among the most spectacular in the movie, and thrilled all the actors, with one exception. David Wenham, as Carl, came to the ball dressed as a colorful court jester. "You don't have to rub it in," comments the actor, "that Van Helsing comes in a beautiful long leather coat and I get stuck in the jester's costume."

Drawings of costume designs by Gabriella Pescucci including everything from Dracula's coat to ball gowns accessorized by Gothic weaponry (right). ABOVE INSET: Dracula in costume. RIGHT INSET: Verona in costume.

CROSSBOWS AND CRUCIFIXES: WEAPONRY

Van Helsing sports innumerable weapons including a Gatling crossbow as imagined in this early drawing (left). In the movie, Carl shows Van Helsing (above) a portion of their Gothic arsenal.

Though the weapons represent a relatively small challenge in the overall scale of this movie, they were no less important to the director than any other aspect of his film. "With every movie I have to come up with new and interesting props and weapons," admits the director. "There's only certain ways you can kill a werewolf or a vampire and we've seen it done. Now I have to take it to the next level."

The designers started with the concept that the only way to kill a vampire is with a stake through his heart and then Sommers added his trademark twist. "What if they are flying around at sixty miles an hour and doing loop-de-loops and circles? Wouldn't it be fun if he had some sort of Gatling gun?" he asked. "And what if the Gatling gun was actually a crossbow gun?"

This was a great idea conceptually and executed with precision by the design group. There was only one problem. Somewhere down the line, someone lost sight of the fact that the weapon had to be carried by an actor while he was running and jumping and diving. No one took into consideration the actual weight of the thing. When the Gatling crossbow arrived on the set in Prague, it weighed about fifty pounds and Hugh Jackman had a difficult time with the hefty prop. Eventually, the weapon was streamlined and made easier to use.

In the movie, it is Carl, played by actor David Wenham

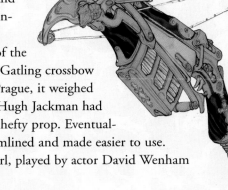

who invents this marvelous contraption, along with many others, and, in one of the opening scenes, he plays "Q" to Jackman's "James Bond," showing him all the toys. "Carl has invented some pretty special weapons," says Wenham. "He invents an explosive called Glycerin 48. Though the film is set in the late 1880s, some of the inventions seem like a mixture of inventions from the 1200s and the 2000s."

Carl has literally created a Van Helsing arsenal. "I have something like 14 weapons in this movie," says Hugh Jackman. "I have guns with silver nitrate bullets. I have a fantastic gas-propelled crossbow. I have a fat gun that has a tether on it so I can swing across moats. I have blow darts and a shotgun. I have rings of garlic, crucifixes, and a flick-knife version of a silver stake. I wear this long coat and I resemble a really bad watch salesmen on 42nd Street because when I open the coat, I have all these weapons attached to the lining."

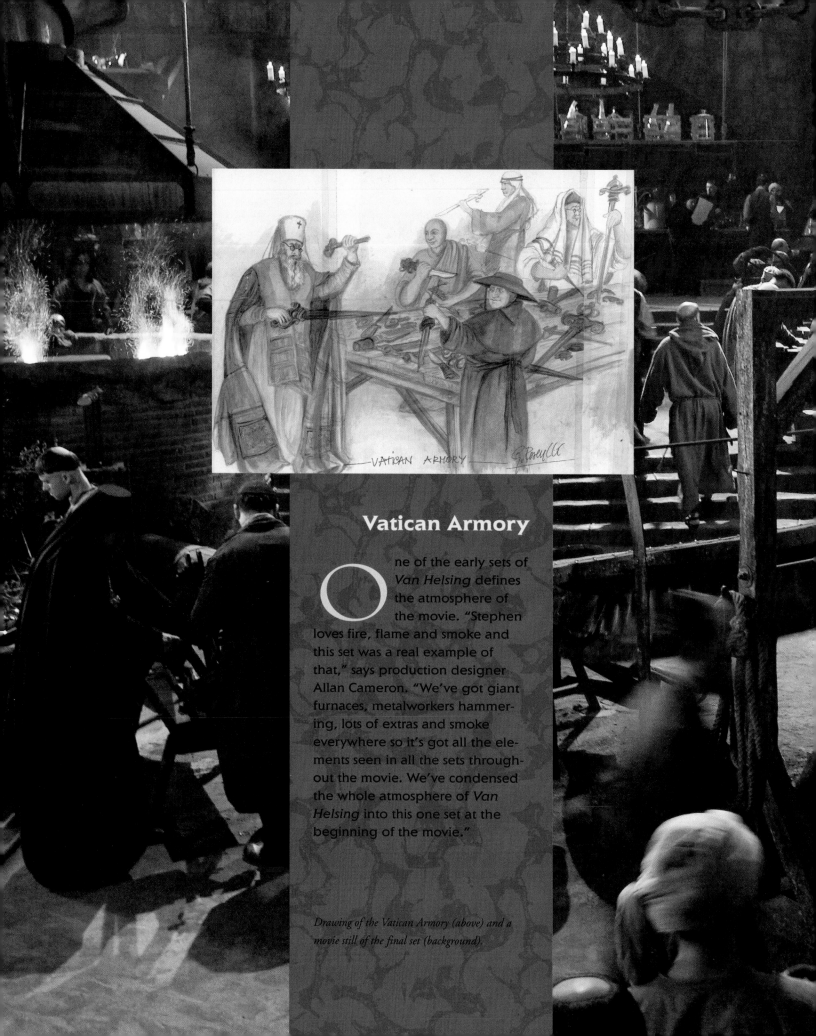

VATICAN ARMORY

Vatican Armory

One of the early sets of *Van Helsing* defines the atmosphere of the movie. "Stephen loves fire, flame and smoke and this set was a real example of that," says production designer Allan Cameron. "We've got giant furnaces, metalworkers hammering, lots of extras and smoke everywhere so it's got all the elements seen in all the sets throughout the movie. We've condensed the whole atmosphere of *Van Helsing* into this one set at the beginning of the movie."

Drawing of the Vatican Armory (above) and a movie still of the final set (background).

Flying Fiends: Stunts

In this digital world of computer-generated images, the job of the stunt coordinator is rapidly changing. "Over the past couple of years, I've repeatedly said that it won't be long before stunt personnel are no longer needed," claims R. A. Rondell, the stunt coordinator for *Van Helsing*. "They are getting really close to replacing people with digital doubles. They haven't quite achieved it yet but it's coming."

In the meantime, Rondell discovered that the workload on this project far exceeded his original expectation. He began, of course, by reviewing the action-packed script. "I was not intimidated by the script," he claims. "I knew it was very ambitious, but I never anticipated being as busy as we were. We worked full out every day, all day long in Prague and then, back in the States, it got even busier."

There was an enormous amount of rigging of the sets which kept Rondell's eight staff members constantly working. Stunt doubles for the cast members were always busy preparing for the shots, rehearsing or doing clean-up. "There was no time for anyone to take breath at all," says Rondell.

Sommers admits that he made it difficult for the stunt team. "All of the people who read the script said that a lot of my ideas were impossible to film. R.A. made almost all of it possible. We made it hard on the stunt team because we were winging stuff all the time. Before this movie, I was afraid of wire work. This isn't a martial arts movie, or a kung fu thing where people are flipping around and flying off the walls. But I wanted to take Hugh Jackman and throw him off the roof of Notre Dame."

Long before shooting began, Rondell met with Hugh Jackman on the set of *X-Men* to assess the actor's skills and capabilities, which is a major part of the stunt coordinator's job. In the end, Rondell determines who does what stunts during the shoot. "It is very important for me to find out where an actor excels and where his weak points may be," he explains. During his initial discussion with Jackman, Rondell needed to find out if the actor had any concerns about the basic stunts in the script. Was he afraid of heights, water or fire? "In Hugh's particular case there weren't any limitations," says Rondell. "He really didn't even need a double except, of course, for insurance purposes."

ABOVE: Aleera (Elena Anaya) on the rooftop before taking flight.
RIGHT: Extensive overhead rigging was used to fly the actors across the set.

> WITH THE THREE BRIDES, THERE WAS A NICE MIX: THE WORLDLY ONE, THE BITCHY ONE, AND THE REALLY CRAZY ONE. EACH OF THEM VIES FOR DRACULA'S ATTENTION. THEN HE GETS INTERESTED IN BITING ME AND THEY ARE INSANELY JEALOUS. IT WAS KIND OF LIKE BEING IN HIGH SCHOOL AGAIN, MAYBE A LITTLE WORSE.
>
> —KATE BECKINSALE

There were times when Rondell prevented Jackman from performing a particular stunt, especially if it involved any danger or risk to the actor. "There are stunt people hired to take risks," explains Rondell. "Not to be cold-hearted, but if a stunt person gets hurt, someone else is waiting to take over. But if an actor gets hurt, there are 300 people who won't get a paycheck and that's unacceptable. The studio relies upon our judgment because even though the audience screams to see the actors performing the action shots, we have to make sure they come to work every day."

Rondell relies on his own assessment of an actor's abilities and not on what he is told. Actors have been known to exaggerate their skills in order to get a part. "To get a part in a film in Australia," confesses actor Richard Roxburgh, "I once lied about my horseback riding abilities which were, at the time, fairly thin. However, I told the filmmakers I was quite accomplished. The day of the shoot, my horse was going berserk and they called action. I thought I was going to die. We were on a precipice with cattle and donkeys. Then I went into this moment when

I was completely the character and he was absolutely fine in the situation. The horse took notice and did what it was told. I got to the other side of it. It's the same with Dracula. When you're in character it's easy. When you feel like, 'I am somebody who walks up a column and then across the roof,' then it makes complete sense to do it. It's a sort of click of the mind."

Work on *Van Helsing* involved a great deal of flying as most of the main characters soar through the air at one time or another. According to Rondell, "Flying is all about rigging and we always use state-of-the-art equipment and professionals with whom I have worked for many, many years. It takes us a day or so to put up the rigs, maybe a day or two of fussing with them and rehearsing. Chad Stahelski, my co-partner, tests the rigs in different harness scenarios to find the most efficient way to go about creating the illusion."

Custom harnesses are made for the actors to wear underneath their clothes. "We can pick them up to whatever elevation we want, travel them across at whatever speed, flip them inside the wires and then drop them down on the ground," says Rondell. "I am most proud of the scene we shot with Hugh and Kate together on the wires. They were 30 or 40 feet in the air, flying across a 70-foot single line. It worked because they trusted us. Trust is the foundation of wirework. If an actor doesn't trust you, he or she will hesitate and their body language will be wrong. Fortunately, both Hugh and Kate were quick studies, good listeners and they trusted us."

> VAN HELSING IS INFUSED WITH MANY OF THE SAME PROBLEMS AND ISSUES AS THE CREATURES THAT HE HUNTS.
>
> —BOB DUCSAY, PRODUCER/EDITOR

Left and Above: Stunts for the actors required various bits of derring-do including jumping from horses and being pulled across the set.

Rondell was equally impressed with Richard Roxburgh's abilities on the wires. "Richard said he could do it and he did it," says Rondell. "I didn't practice much with him. He showed me he was comfortable, right off the bat, and just stepped right into it. So that was really easy."

The actor enjoyed his time in the air. "I love hanging from the rafters and walking across the ceiling," Roxburgh says, and then adds, "I'd get a real buzz out of hanging upside down, if it wasn't for the pressure headaches."

In addition to the actors flying on *Van Helsing*, the cameras also had to fly. On a set the length of two football fields, cameras were attached to wire rigging and could move at about fifty miles an hour.

"There was one scene where the brides were attacking," says Jackman, "and they're using this big camera that's swinging around everywhere. Steve said, 'Okay, I'm going to let everybody loose. No matter what happens, just keep running. I'll pick whichever footage I like.' The camera followed me wherever I went and it was sheer mayhem. In the first few seconds, I knocked over this old woman. I immediately went to pick her up and Steve called cut. 'Mate,' he said, 'I know you knocked someone over but this is a big shot. You just keep running and I'll edit it.' We did four takes and someone counted: I knocked over fifteen people, just laid them out. Men, women, children, gone. Stephen was screaming behind the monitor, 'Run, Hugh, run! Don't apologize to the old woman.'"

My favorite line in the script was when I say to Marishka,
'Never trust a man to do a woman's job.' It's so true!

—Silvia Colloca, Verona

Flying

During the course of the story, the brides transform from fully gowned women to flying harpies. Their long flowing sleeves change into wings as their clothes are absorbed into their skin. The animators studied films of bats flying and mantas swimming underwater to replicate the movement of their wings. "We wanted to create unstructured wings," says Ben Snow, ILM visual effects supervisor. "We looked at manta ray footage and got excited by the idea of this amorphous wing that could be stiff and have the structure of flying but could also drape."

ABOVE LEFT: Dracula sends Aleera and Verona to do his bidding. ABOVE: The Brides' aerial attack on the village. BELOW: Concept drawing of the transformation of the brides.

Terrifying Transformations: Visual Effects

LEFT: Visual effects shots of The Wolf Man.
BELOW: Visual effects shot of Frankenstein's Monster.

The visual effects supervisor works with the director in pre-production, examining the script to determine which shots are visual effects that will be completed after filming. Then his job is to supervise all aspects of creating those effects. *Van Helsing* was such a big production that two visual effects supervisors, Scott Squires and Ben Snow, worked together on the movie. "It was a pretty big show," Scott Squires admits. "We had more than 500 shots that needed our participation." The job took more than two years and required the work of more than one hundred effects artists. "There were a lot of difficult visual effects to do and they had to be combined with a lot of difficult stunt work and special effects work on set," explains Snow.

Visual effects were needed for all the transformations: Dr. Jekyll and Mr. Hyde, the Hellbeast, the brides and especially The Wolf Man. "We had to combine the actor's heads with their computer generated bodies and that made it particularly challenging," says Squires.

The first step in creating any of those transformations was to work out the initial design of the creatures. "Every time you see a werewolf," says Squires, "he will be computer generated. So we worked out the design and then we went through a number of research and development projects to simulate how that would look."

Three werewolves were created for the movie. The major Wolf Man is a featured character and had to be shot up-close. "The Wolf Man is a hero character and the audience has to completely believe in him," explains Snow. "He has to act, he has to look angry and scared and emote a great deal. He also has to transform from Will Kemp into the wolf character. The transformation is very elaborate and requires a lot of animation and technical work to blend the two bodies. In the film, we have the actors virtually tear themselves out of their skin."

The visual effects team was greatly inspired by the work of actor Will Kemp. "Will's acting was so intense," says Snow, "it looked like he was willing himself to transform into a wolf. It was great to watch."

These transformations involved creating human skin, hair and fur, as well as water, some of the most difficult effects to achieve. "We had some scenes where the Wolf Man was coming in out of the rain so we had to generate a wet look of hair," says Squires. "The long, flowing hair on the three brides was also a big challenge. The effects had to match the actual live action of the brides." New software was created to develop these looks.

The team put a huge amount of effort into creating Hellbeast, the alter-ego for Dracula. "The Hellbeast was a very important character to the director," says Snow. "Stephen wanted him to be very unique and different from anything previously seen on film. We looked at all sorts of different concepts."

While many of the monsters in the movie retain some of the look of the actor playing him, Hellbeast was a different sort of animal. "We took Richard Roxburgh and completely transformed him into this beast from hell," explains Snow.

In addition to creating an effect that matches the actor, the team had to match the movement of the camera. "In Stephen's movies, the camera is always moving," Squires explains. "We have to go back on the computer and make a computer camera that matches that exact motion. No matter what we add to the scene, it has to look like it was there originally. That really is key to the process."

In all, the job of creating the computer generated monsters for *Van Helsing* was an incredibly complex task that melded classic horror figures with modern technology. "It was a very tricky thing to pull off," admits Snow. "Once you've established this universe of Hellbeasts and vampires and werewolves, you try to keep it fairly realistic within that context."

It is almost impossible to calculate the number of hours and the amount of work done by the visual effects department. Depending on the complexity of any given scene, the team often spent months on a single shot. Ironically, in the finished movie, that scene might only last for fifteen or twenty seconds on the screen.

> I WAS NEVER NERVOUS WHEN WE WERE SHOOTING ON THE BURNING WOODEN STRUCTURE. IT WAS A CONTROLLED FIRE. AT LEAST I THINK IT WAS.
>
> —SHULER HENSLEY, FRANKENSTEIN'S MONSTER

CLOCKWISE FROM TOP LEFT: Special effects included the flying vampire bride, Dracula's transformation, Van Helsing's journey through the mirror, and the Frankenstein Monster's encounter with fire.

Mixing Genres: Post-Production

Bob Ducsay is both the producer and the editor of *Van Helsing*, two titles which represent an unusual combination of skills and talents. Ducsay and Sommers have been working together for more than fifteen years and their collaboration is a key element of the filming making process. Ducsay started his career as a picture editor but his interests in filmmaking were always far–reaching. Over the years, he and Sommers have created a unique working relationship.

Their collaboration always begins at the very start of the movie, in pre-production, which lasted for close to a year on *Van Helsing*. "We solved a lot of problems going in," says Ducsay, "but when we started shooting the movie there were many unresolved issues that we had to address over the course of making the film."

The shoot schedule for *Van Helsing* lasted for seven months, with 108 days of shooting. By any standard in the film business, that was an extremely long period of time to keep the cameras rolling. One of the challenges in such a long and arduous shoot was to keep the momentum going because, no matter how exhausted the cast and crew, whatever was shot on day 108 was as important as what was shot on day one. Sommers and Ducsay tried to conquer this problem by making the process as stress-free as possible and by creating an environment that kept spirits up and people focused.

"We think that it's essential to create a positive environment and we surround ourselves with the sort of people who enjoy what they do," says Ducsay. "We've all worked on films where the environment is unpleasant, where the studio is unpleasant, where the whole process of making the movie becomes a grind. I don't know why anyone would want to create an environment that is negative and difficult."

For the director, surrounding himself with people he enjoys is crucial. "Several movies ago, I came to realize that my kind of film is very hard to make," Sommers explains. "We're either shooting in the sweltering Sahara Desert or knee-deep in snow in Eastern Europe. At the same time, we're dealing with all these mechanical and special effects

RIGHT: Bob Ducsay, left, discusses a scene with director Stephen Sommers.

that make the shoot even more strenuous. I decided that I just did not want to make it any harder by working with difficult people. And I haven't. I've been very lucky."

Ducsay thinks it is more than just luck. "Stephen brings an enormous sense of joy and enthusiasm to the set which translates to the actors and, in the end, I think it shows up on the screen," says the producer.

It is very expensive to re-shoot scenes once production has wrapped so these filmmakers work hard to get their entire film while they are still shooting. "I think some directors always have it in the back of their minds that they are going to go back and re-shoot things anyway, so it doesn't really much matter if they get it the first time," explains Ducsay. "Stephen's mentality is 'I want this movie finished when we're done with principal photography.' My input during shooting inevitably helps in post-production. I am able to assist in the sense that I can see if there's a piece of coverage missing that we can shoot during production. In the end, this has saved us a lot of time and effort. On our last two films, we have not had to go back to re-shoot in post-production. This is very unusual for the kinds of big films that we are making."

According to Ducsay, the single most difficult challenge of editing a film like *Van Helsing* is bringing a consistent tone on a minute-by-minute basis, to a movie that combines so many genres. "Stephen and I love making movies that are mixed genre," explains Ducsay. "We've got horror, comedy, romance, action, and adventure. One minute someone is screaming in terror and the next minute they are laughing. These elements often work against one another. You can have everyone really frightened in a scene but if you bring in a joke too early, it subverts the tension. And vice versa. We try to resolve these issues in the script stage. We would look at certain places in the story and ask if this was the right time to have a joke. In the end, though, when you can make it work, it's the most satisfying thing you can possibly do."

Post-production on *Van Helsing* continued for an entire year after principal photography because of all the special effects work.

WE ARE ALL FASCINATED WITH THE DARK SIDE, WITH DEATH, GHOSTS, MONSTERS AND CHAOS. THIS HAS BEEN THE STUFF OF FICTION AND OF CAMPFIRE STORIES FOR HUNDREDS OF YEARS AND IT ALWAYS WILL BE.

—HUGH JACKMAN

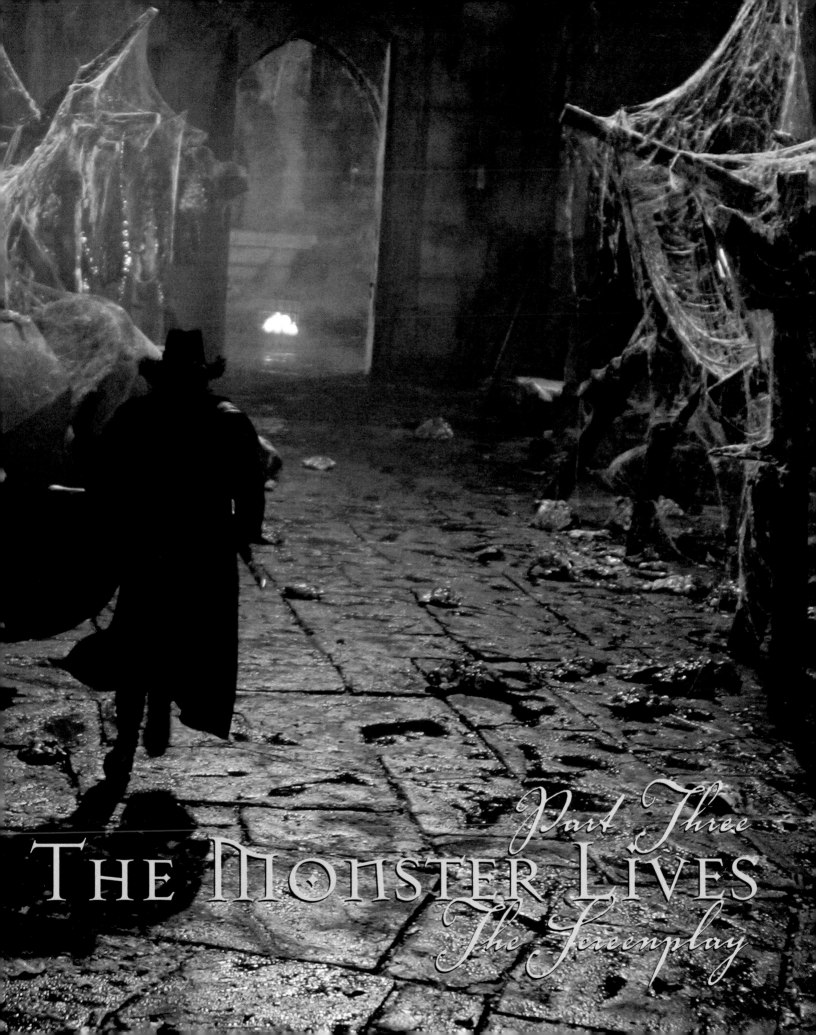

Part Three
THE MONSTER LIVES
The Screenplay

EXT. FOREST – NIGHT
LIGHTNING FLASHES across the OLD UNIVERSAL LOGO. And then a FLAMING TORCH BURNS IT AWAY and we find ourselves in the middle of an angry mob of torch-wielding PEASANTS. Crashing through a dark forest. Heading for a huge CASTLE. A BOLT OF LIGHTNING STRIKES conductors above the skylight on top of the castle. —This entire opening sequence is in BLACK & WHITE.

INT. LABORATORY – NIGHT
A PAIR OF STRANGE EYES suddenly comes alive, peering out through slits in stained bandages.

A MAN spins around into a CLOSE-UP, his elegant face is covered in soot, sweat, and taut lines of exhaustion. But his eyes sparkle with an incredible intelligence, bordering on madness. This is DOCTOR VICTOR FRANKEN-STEIN. He yells one of the most famous phrases in film history:

> **VICTOR**
> He's alive. . . . He's alive!! . . . HE'S ALIIIIVE!!!

Behind him, lying in a form-fitted iron pod, is a huge man, face covered in bandages. A loud CRASH spins Victor around, he runs to a window and looks out. Over his shoulder we see the mob charge the front gate with a tree trunk— CRASH! Wood SPLINTERS. But the gate holds. Victor starts to panic, he spins around and comes face-to-face with a DARK FIGURE.

> **DRACULA** (Dark Figure)
> Success!!

Victor SCREAMS in fright, then catches himself.

> **VICTOR**
> Oh . . . Count . . . it's just you.

The Dark Figure steps forward into the flickering electrical light-show. Tall, dark, and incredibly handsome, he reeks of evil. This is COUNT VLADISLAUS DRACULA.

> **DRACULA**
> I was beginning to lose faith, Victor.

He looks out at the screaming mob.

> **DRACULA** (cont'd)
> A pity your moment of triumph is being spoiled over a little thing like grave robbery.

EXT. CASTLE FRANKENSTEIN – NIGHT
A creepy guy in a TOP HAT and under-taker's suit YELLS OUT:

> **TOP HAT**
> You know what he's doing in there! To the bodies of your loved ones!

INT. LABORATORY – NIGHT
Victor is clearly on the verge of a nervous breakdown.

> **VICTOR**
> I must . . . I must escape this place.

Victor dashes across his laboratory; the Industrial Age at its grotesque beginnings. Weird iron generators and enormous cop-per dynamos line the walls. Huge gears GRIND. Massive fan belts WHIRL. Electricity ARCS everywhere. Dracula is now high up in the rafters, as if magically transported.

> **DRACULA**
> Where are you going to run, Victor?

SPARKS rain down as Victor throws open a traveling chest and wildly begins pack-ing. Dracula is suddenly on the complete opposite side of the room, pacing the mantelpiece.

> **DRACULA** (cont'd)
> Your peculiar experiments have made you . . . unwelcome, in most of the civilized world.

Victor looks up at Dracula, momentarily confused by Dracula's impossible moves.

> **VICTOR**
> I'll take him away, far away, where no one will ever find him.

He starts packing again, but Dracula is

suddenly right next to him. He steps on the lid of the trunk and slams it shut.

DRACULA
No, Victor, the time has come for me to take command of him.

VICTOR
What are you saying?

DRACULA
Why do you think I brought you here? Gave you this castle? Equipped your lab?

VICTOR
You said you believed in my work.

DRACULA
And I do. But now that it is, as you yourself said, "a triumph of science over god," it must now serve my purpose.

VICTOR
What purpose?

EXT. CASTLE FRANKENSTEIN – NIGHT
WHAM! goes the tree trunk. Splinters FLY. The gate starts to give. The Crowd CHEERS. Thunder ROARS.

INT. LABORATORY – NIGHT
Victor's eyes slowly widen in horror, he starts to back away.

VICTOR
Good lord . . . I would kill myself before helping in such a task.

DRACULA
Feel free. I don't actually need you anymore, Victor. I just need him . . . he is the key.

Dracula moves in for the kill. Victor backs away towards the roaring fireplace, eyes narrowing in defiance.

VICTOR
Before I would allow him to be used for such evil, I would destroy him.

DRACULA
I cannot allow that to happen. My brides would be very put out.

VICTOR
IGOR! . . . Help me!

A despicable little hunchback with horrible buck teeth and an evil eye stares down from the rafters. This is IGOR.

IGOR
You have been so kind to me, Doctor, so caring and thoughtful. *(gestures out to the mob)* But if they catch me, they'll hang me again.

Igor reveals his horribly disfigured and broken neck. Victor quickly reaches above the mantel and grabs a sabre crossed over the Frankenstein family coat-of-arms.

VICTOR
Stay back!

DRACULA
You can't kill me, Victor . . .

Dracula impales himself on Victor's sabre and keeps walking, impaling himself all the way up to the hilt, bringing the two men eye-to-eye. Victor is beyond shocked. Dracula smiles.

DRACULA *(cont'd)*
. . . I'm *already* dead.

EXT. CASTLE FRANKENSTEIN – NIGHT
CRASH! goes the front gate. EXPLODING into splinters. Peasants and torches pour through. LIGHTNING FLASHES.

INT. LABORATORY – NIGHT
Dracula's canines glide out into razor sharp fangs, all the blood drains from his face, his hair turns pure white. Victor SCREAMS. The Count bites down into his neck.

Up in the rafters, Igor scurries off through a door, slamming it behind him as Victor's SHADOW is murdered above it.

Dracula drops Victor's limp body to the floor. And that's when a horrific ANGUISHED BELLOW suddenly fills the room.

FRANKENSTEIN
NOOO!

Dracula spins around, dropping Victor to the floor. A dynamo hits Dracula full on. He and the dynamo are flung into the fireplace, scattering flaming logs and embers.

A bandaged APPARITION scoops Victor up into its arms.

EXT. CASTLE FRANKENSTEIN – NIGHT
Igor scurries out a small door outside the castle wall and closes it behind him, then he looks up over the wall to the peasants storming the upper ramparts. He cackles in glee. The door behind him suddenly bursts open. The Apparition races out, carrying Victor in its arms. It blows past Igor and heads off across the moors, heading for an old WINDMILL up on a bluff. Igor is shocked and panicked, he quickly looks up at the peasants and points to the Apparition.

> **IGOR**
> FRANKENSTEIN! He's created a monster!!

Igor fearfully scurries off into the shadows.

EXT. RAMPART – NIGHT
Up on the ramparts, Top Hat points down and SCREAMS:

> **TOP HAT**
> LOOK! It's headed for the windmill!

INT. LABORATORY – NIGHT
From inside the fireplace, the Count flings the massive dynamo across the laboratory. It hits a generator that blasts into a flume of sparks and fire. The Count charges out of the fireplace, his face is a burned mess, *but it quickly and completely heals.*

EXT. WINDMILL – NIGHT
The mob charges across the moors, chasing the Apparition towards the windmill.

INT. WINDMILL – NIGHT
The mob charges the windmill. The creature slams the door shut on them, then dashes across the room, which is an old *Absinthe Still.* He rampages up a rickety wooden staircase.

EXT. TOP OF WINDMILL – NIGHT
At the top of the windmill, the creature rages through a splintering door and looks down at the crazed mob below. We finally get our first good look at FRANKENSTEIN'S MONSTER: bolts, scars, stitches, and the back of his head is

made of glass, *a small electrical storm is going off inside it.* But the look in his eyes surprises us, he is terrified, this tremendous beast of a man is actually fearful.

> **FRANKENSTEIN**
> Why? . . .

INT. LABORATORY – NIGHT
Dracula's SHADOW rises up the laboratory walls and TRANSFORMS into something huge, *with wings.*

EXT. TOP OF WINDMILL – NIGHT
Frankenstein groans in fear as a thick unbroken band of FLICKERING TORCHES encircles the windmill. The SCREAMING peasants throw their torches. A noose of FLAME leaps up the walls. The Monster ROARS. Then looks off at the castle. Off in the distance, the castle's glass skylight bursts as a WINGED SHADOW explodes up out of it. High up in the dark, thunder-racked sky, THREE MORE liquid-like SHADOWS come flying through the roiling purple clouds to join it.

> **PEASANTS**
> Vampires! Run for your lives!

The huge crowd flees in horror across the moors. The FLAMES have surged up the windmill and now surround Frankenstein's Monster. He looks down at Victor and hugs him tightly to his chest.

> **FRANKENSTEIN**
> Father . . .

Then with tears on his cheeks, he lifts a fist towards the oncoming shadows above and lets out an anguished BELLOW.

And that's when the entire windmill IMPLODES. Taking the Monster and his creator down with it. The timber and the gears and the fans and all the ironwork plummet downward. A huge ball of FIRE and FLAMING DEBRIS flies everywhere.

Huge billowing WINGS suddenly fly right over CAMERA, practically WIPING FRAME. They immediately become a CAPE, which wraps around Dracula as he hits the ground running.

And then three billowing WHITE WINGS fly over CAMERA, and they wrap around three exotically gorgeous young women. Dracula's BRIDES: ALEERA, VERONA, and MARISHKA.

Dracula staggers to a stop and stares in desperation at the flaming wreckage. His Brides are distraught beyond words: they burst into tears, wailing with inhuman shrieks.

WE PUSH IN on the FLAMING windmill, belching its last sparks, then slowly DISSOLVE TO its charred remains.

SUPER: ONE YEAR LATER

EXT. WINDMILL – DAY
The BLACK & WHITE ends, the FILM SATURATES, becoming a deep blue, and then a huge, powerful BLUR rips past the ruins. The sound it makes is incredibly deep, feral, and frightening.

EXT. FOREST CLEARING – GLOOMY DAY
Looking down through MASSIVE TREES onto a small clearing. A handsome young MAN is tied to a post, hands above his head. PRINCE VELKAN tenses at the sound of the approaching beast. And then all goes quiet. Bushes rustle. Velkan's eyes look left. A tree creaks. Velkan looks right. A branch sways. Velkan waits for the inevitable. And then, 30 feet up a tree, a massive WEREWOLF creeps out, clinging horizontally to the bark. Ten feet tall. Fangs. Claws. The works. It hunches, about to lunge. Velkan tenses.

> **VELKAN**
> Come on. Dracula unleashed you for a reason.

The Werewolf leaps. Velkan's hands rip loose of his bindings. He vaults himself up onto the top of the post just as the Werewolf slams into it, just missing him. The Werewolf clings to the post and looks up as Velkan leaps up and grabs a vine hanging above the post.

BEHIND SOME BUSHES: Several MEN pull a lever.

The vine jerks Velkan up off the pole, heading for safety, but then he comes to an abrupt stop. The look in his eyes tells us this isn't part of the plan.

Behind the bushes the men are struggling with the lever.

VILLAGER
It's stuck! It's stuck!

A gorgeous young woman spins around and draws her sword: she wears the sexy silk dress of a gypsy Princess, this is ANNA VALERIOUS. One of the men grabs her.

MAN
No! Anna! It will kill you!

ANNA (ripping free of his grip)
That's my brother out there!

Out in the clearing, the Werewolf snarls up at Velkan and starts to hunch, about to lunge up at him. Anna charges out of the bushes. The Werewolf sees her. So does Velkan.

VELKAN
Anna! No!

Anna raises her sword and keeps on charging. The Werewolf snarls viciously and

jumps off the pole, it immediately falls through a camouflaged mesh covering the ground.

Behind the bushes a man swings an ax and chops the ropes attached to the lever.

Out in the clearing, a huge iron CAGE rips up out of the ground around the pole. Anna does a back-flip off the cage as it's pulled up into the air.

Up on the vine, Velkan draws his silver revolver. The roof of the cage springs shut, trapping the Werewolf inside. Velkan aims down at the Werewolf, but the cage slams into him on it's way up into the trees. His revolver goes flying. Velkan and the cage are rocketed straight up into the huge trees.

EXT. FOREST – TREETOPS – DAY
Way up in the trees, the cage slams to a stop. Velkan leaps off and lands on a branch. The cage starts crashing back and forth, the Werewolf trying to rip its way out. Ropes snap.

VELKAN
My gun! Find my gun!

EXT. FOREST – CLEARING – DAY
Down in the clearing, Anna desperately

looks around, several men begin firing rifles up into the trees, Anna shoves one of them out of her way.

ANNA
No! Find Velkan's gun! It has to be the silver bullets!

EXT. FOREST – TREETOPS – DAY
Another rope snaps. The cage swings wildly, now hanging by a single rope.

EXT. FOREST – CLEARING – DAY
Anna spots Velkan's silver revolver on the far side of the clearing. She runs for it. The cage suddenly SLAMS DOWN right in front of her, cutting her off from the gun. The Werewolf bursts out of the smashed cage. Anna turns and runs like hell. The Werewolf spots her and gives chase.

Anna races through the foliage. The Werewolf's POV getting closer and closer. Anna runs out of the forest and almost goes over a cliff. She stops herself just short, it's a half mile to the bottom, she spins around and starts to run back into the foliage, then freezes as she sees trees and bushes thrown into the air, the Werewolf getting closer and closer. The Werewolf leaps out of the bushes, straight at Anna. Anna is suddenly shoved out of the way by Velkan. He fires his gun. The Werewolf HOWLS in pain, but manages to chomp into Velkan's shoulder and tackle him OFF THE SCREEN.

Anna slams to the ground, then spins around, Velkan and the Werewolf are gone. Only the revolver remains, still smoking. Anna leaps up and looks over the edge of the misty cliff. Velkan is nowhere in sight. Anna is devastated.

ANNA
Velkan . . .

And then she hears something and spins around. It's the Werewolf, lying in the bushes. Anna grabs the gun, levels it, cocks it, and moves in for the kill. And that's when the Werewolf TRANSFORMS, turning into a dying OLD MAN.

OLD MAN
Thank you.

Anna stares down at him, horrified. The Old Man smiles.

> **OLD MAN** *(cont'd)*
> I die free from Dracula's awful grip.

And then with the last of his energy he grabs Anna's ankle.

> **OLD MAN** *(cont'd)*
> But now you must stop him! . . . He has a terrible secret. . . . He has . . . he has . . . !

The Old Man dies. Anna stares down at him, then looks off over the precipice. WE PUSH IN on her tear-streaked face as she shuts her eyes. Then PULL BACK as another FACE DISSOLVES UP over hers. It's a "WANTED POSTER." Wanted for murder in many countries is a MASKED MAN wearing a cloak, a cape, and a black, wide-brimmed hat. His name is VAN HELSING. A HAND rips the poster off the SCREEN and we suddenly find ourselves in:

PARIS, FRANCE – RAINY NIGHT
The hand belongs to a masked man in a cloak, a cape, and a black, wide-brimmed hat. In the background is the Eiffel Tower, half built. It's quiet. Too quiet. And then we hear a blood curdling SCREAM. Van Helsing's eyes don't even flinch, he calmly crumples the poster, chucks it, and moves off down the foggy cobblestone lane, his cape flowing behind him.

EXT. NOTRE DAME – NIGHT
WE PAN DOWN from NOTRE DAME to a WOMAN'S DEAD BODY lying on the cobblestones in a puddle of blood, eyes wide open, looking terrified. Van Helsing steps up and gives the body the once over, studying the spoor. He picks up a smoldering cigar stub next to the body, dripping with saliva, then he freezes, eyes suddenly on the alert, he spins around and we RACK FOCUS to the top of Notre Dame.

Way up on the North Tower, a huge, shadowy FIGURE clambers up the sheer wall and vanishes over an upper railing.

INT. NOTRE DAME BELFRY – NIGHT
Van Helsing silently steps up into the belfry, which is dark and dusty and covered in religious relics. Very Gothic. Moonlight slices through the attic windows as Van Helsing glides past the massive church bell, then he freezes, every hair and muscle on his body suddenly tense. A long BEAT.

And then a gigantic malformed MAN DROPS DOWN three feet in front of him, hanging upside-down from the rafters. He SNARLS viciously. This is MISTER HYDE. Van Helsing gingerly takes one step back, then pulls down his mask, revealing his handsome face for the first time.

> **VAN HELSING**
> Evening.

Hyde's fleshy jowls spew phlegm as he speaks, a burning cigar clamped between his rotten teeth.

> **MISTER HYDE**
> You're a big one. You'll be hard to digest.

> **VAN HELSING**
> I'd hate to be such a nuisance.

Hyde flips around and lands on his gnarled feet. Van Helsing sizes him up, all nine feet of him.

> **VAN HELSING** *(cont'd)*
> I missed you in London.

> **MISTER HYDE**
> No you didn't.

Hyde lifts up his huge arm to show three cauterized BULLET HOLES blown clear through his biceps.

> **MISTER HYDE** *(cont'd)*
> You got me good.

Hyde starts to circle. Van Helsing does likewise.

> **VAN HELSING**
> Doctor Jekyll, you are wanted by the Knights of the Holy Order—

> **MISTER HYDE**
> It's Mister Hyde now.

> **VAN HELSING**
> —for the murder of twelve men, six women—

> **MISTER HYDE**
> —Four children, three goats, and a rather nasty massacre of poultry. So you're the great Van Helsing.

He blows a huge smoke ring at Van Helsing. Van Helsing ignores it.

> **VAN HELSING**
> And you are a deranged psychopath.

Hyde takes the red-hot cigar out of his mouth and crushes the glowing end into his palm.

> **MISTER HYDE**
> We all have our little problems.

Van Helsing's whole mind and body start to gear up.

> **VAN HELSING**
> My superiors would like for me to take you alive, so that they may extricate your better half.

> **MISTER HYDE**
> They would, would they?

> **VAN HELSING**
> Personally, I'd rather just kill you and call it a day.

Mister Hyde laughs. Van Helsing doesn't.

> **VAN HELSING** *(cont'd)*
> Let's make it *your* decision, shall we?

Hyde suddenly LASHES OUT with one of his huge hands, catches Van Helsing across the face, slams him back into a wall. Van Helsing calmly wipes the blood off his mouth.

> **VAN HELSING** *(cont'd)*
> Good, we're in agreement then.

In a lightning quick move, Van Helsing draws his revolvers and FIRES. Like all of Van Helsing's weapons, they are highly stylized, yet ruthlessly functional. The sound is thunderous. As the smoke clears,

Hyde is nowhere to be seen. Van Helsing holsters his guns and moves forward. Mister Hyde suddenly charges out of the darkness. Van Helsing instantly comes up with circular BLADES in each hand. He spins around and cuts Hyde across the ribs as he passes. Hyde howls in pain and, unable to stop his own momentum, crashes straight into the huge church BELL, which GONGS loudly. Hyde grabs his ears.

MISTER HYDE
The bell! THE BELL!!

Van Helsing moves in for the kill. His fingers start pumping the spring-loaded blades, which begin to rotate, faster and faster until they're a menacing blur of razor sharp steel.

Hyde grabs the huge bell, rips it off its moorings and slams it down over Van Helsing, trapping him inside. Hyde chuckles. And then he hears the blades buzzing away inside. Hyde looks concerned, grabs the bell, and lifts it up. Van Helsing is gone, and there's a big hole carved out of the wooden floor.

Hyde scowls, then hears the blades buzzing again. He looks around. Van Helsing is nowhere in sight, then he looks up. Van Helsing is crouched up inside the bell above Hyde's head. He swings a blade. *Mister Hyde's left arm drops to the floor.* Cut clean off. The bell crashes to the floor. Van Helsing rolls free. He and Hyde stare at the severed arm, flapping away on the floor.

VAN HELSING
I'll bet that's upsetting.

The huge arm TRANSFORMS into the arm of a spindly old man. Mister Hyde angrily lunges forward, grabs Van Helsing, and throws him clear up through the top of the tower.

EXT. NORTH TOWER – NIGHT
Van Helsing explodes up through a wooden trap door and crashes down hard to the deck. He tries to get up, but he's nearly unconscious. Hyde leaps up beside him, picks him up by the back of his collar and carries him across the tower.

MISTER HYDE
I think you'll find the view over here rather spectacular.

At the edge of the tower, Hyde lifts Van Helsing up face-to-face.

MISTER HYDE *(cont'd)*
Been a pleasure knowing you.

Mister Hyde throws Van Helsing off the

top of Notre Dame. OKAY, EVERY-THING HAPPENS AT ONCE, PAY CLOSE ATTENTION:

As Van Helsing plummets towards the cobblestones far below he desperately whips out a grappling hook gun, *aims*, and fires it upwards. The bolt shoots out, tether trailing behind it. It blows right through Hyde's belly and shoots out of his back.

TIGHT on the bolt as it slows in mid-air, tether slackening, and then the serrated grappling HOOKS snap out, the tether goes taut, and the whole thing is jerked back out of FRAME.

The grappling hooks slam into Mister Hyde's back. The tether goes taut. Van Helsing snaps to a stop at the end of the tether, two feet short of splattering into the cobblestones. Hyde is jerked forward, but catches himself on the ledge. Van Helsing gets to his feet, grabs the tether and yanks it. Hyde is jerked over the edge, but a single toe stops him from falling, his lone arm flails, and

then with all his might he throws himself backwards. READ FASTER:

Van Helsing is jerked up off the ground. Hyde stumbles back and falls off the rear of the tower, he drops down and crashes through the roof of the church. Van Helsing rockets up the side of Notre Dame, heading for the top of the tower.

INT. NOTRE DAME – NIGHT
Mister Hyde swings down across the great church and right into the Rose window.

EXT. NOTRE DAME – NIGHT
The massive window at the front and center of Notre Dame explodes as Mister Hyde crashes through it. Van Helsing lands on his feet at the top of the tower and looks down.

WE FOLLOW Mister Hyde down as he TRANSFORMS into a meek OLD MAN, who has one deeply disturbing moment to consider his predicament. And then he hits the pavement.

Up on the tower, Van Helsing looks genuinely remorseful, his body slumps in sadness, he makes the sign-of-the-cross.

> **VAN HELSING**
> God rest your soul. . . .

EXT. PLAZA – NIGHT
Gendarmes, priests, and local denizens race up to the dead body from every direction. Then they all look up to the top of the North Tower, *and are instantly terrified*, several of them run away in fear.

> **PEOPLE**
> Van Helsing! . . . It's Van Helsing! . . .

Silhouetted against the moon is our hero. The SERGEANT of the gendarmes raises an angry fist.

> **SERGEANT** *(O.S.)*
> Van Helsing you MURDERERRRR . . . !!

SMASH CUT TO ROME – DAWN
The clock behind St. Peter's Basilica chimes as Van Helsing trots his black

stallion across the enormous Piazza San Pietro, lined with Bernini's magnificent colonnades.

SUPER: VATICAN CITY

INT. ST. PETERS – DAWN
Gregorian CHANTING can be heard as Van Helsing strides through the greatest church in all Christendom.

INT. CONFESSIONAL – DAY
Inside an ornate confessional, Van Helsing drops to one knee.

> **VAN HELSING**
> Bless me, Father, for I have sinned.

Knowing what's coming, Van Helsing grits his teeth. A tiny partition door slams open. Through the wooden mesh we see CARDINAL JINETTE, a tough old bird with piercing eyes.

> **CARDINAL JINETTE**
> You shattered the Rose window!

> **VAN HELSING**
> Not to split hairs, sir, but it was Mister Hyde who did the shattering.

> **THIRTEEN**
> Thirteenth-century. Over six hundred years old! I wish you a week in hell for that!

> **VAN HELSING**
> It would be a nice reprieve.

> **CARDINAL JINETTE**
> Don't get me wrong, your results are unquestionable, but your methods draw far too much attention. "Wanted posters"? We are not pleased.

> **VAN HELSING**
> You think I like being the most wanted man in Europe? Why don't you and the Order do something about it?

The Cardinal leans in and lowers his voice conspiratorially.

> **CARDINAL JINETTE**
> You know why, because "we" do not exist.

> **VAN HELSING**
> Then neither do I.

Van Helsing gets up to go. The Cardinal pulls a lever. Bolts on Van Helsing's door lock shut. The Cardinal leans in, all fire and brimstone.

> **CARDINAL JINETTE**
> When we found you crawling up the steps of this church, half dead, it was clear to all of us that you had been sent to do God's work.

> **VAN HELSING**
> Why can't he do it himself?

> **CARDINAL JINETTE**
> Don't blaspheme! You already lost your memory as a penance for past sins.

The Cardinal pulls another lever, a series of gears slides the back wall open, revealing a secret hidden staircase.

> **CARDINAL JINETTE** (cont'd)
> If you wish to recover it, I suggest you continue to heed the call.

INT. ARMORY – DAY
The Cardinal and Van Helsing enter an enormous underground ARMORY, bustling with action, lots of steam and fire.

> **CARDINAL JINETTE**
> Governments and empires come and go, but we have kept mankind safe since time immemorial.

Beneath the giant blast furnaces we see JEWISH RABBIS working the billows, HINDU PRIESTS stoking the fires, and MUSLIM CLERICS hammering red hot scimitars on anvils.

> **CARDINAL JINETTE** (cont'd)
> We are the last defense against evil. An evil that the rest of Mankind has no idea even exists.

Van Helsing's eyes fill with torment, reliving past moments:

> **VAN HELSING**
> To you, these monsters are evil beings to be vanquished, but I'm the one left standing there when they die and become the men they once were.

> **CARDINAL JINETTE**
> For you, my good son, this is all a test of faith. That is why you have no idea who you are or where you came from.

Van Helsing gives him a look. The Cardinal smiles knowingly.

CARDINAL JINETTE (cont'd)
Say you met God, and he set you on a task, you would have no fear because you would know that God was with you, but if your memory of meeting God were lost, then every day would be a test of faith.

Van Helsing sighs heavily, we see the weariness in his eyes, the weight of his calling pressing down upon him. The Cardinal snaps his fingers and the LIGHT DIMS. A Rabbi turns on a SLIDE PROJECTOR and starts clicking slides, showing the way from Rome to Eastern Europe.

CARDINAL JINETTE (cont'd)
We need you to go to the east, to the far side of Romania, an accursed land, terrorized by all sorts of night-marish creatures.

A slide of a handsome GOTHIC PRINCE comes up.

CARDINAL JINETTE (cont'd)
Lorded over by a certain Count Dracula.

Van Helsing's interest is immediately piqued.

VAN HELSING
Dracula.

Then a slide comes up showing a painting of an old fifteenth-century NOBLEMAN, his suit of armor covered in holy crosses, his name emblazoned on silver below it: VALERIOUS THE ELDER.

CARDINAL JINETTE
Four hundred and fifty years ago a Transylvanian knight named Valerious the Elder promised God that his family would never rest, nor enter heaven, until they vanquished Dracula from their land. They have not succeeded, and they are running out of family.

Several grainy black-and-white slides of a FAMILY come up. A burly old KING and young Prince Velkan.

CARDINAL JINETTE (cont'd)
Boris Valerious, King of the Gypsies, he went missing almost one year ago. His son Velkan died just last week.

VAN HELSING
And the girl?

Van Helsing gestures to Anna, riding her horse.

CARDINAL JINETTE
Princess Anna, the last of the Valerious. If she is killed, nine generations of her family will never enter the gates of St. Peter.

The room FLOODS WITH LIGHT. The Cardinal faces Van Helsing.

CARDINAL JINETTE (cont'd)
For more than four centuries this family has held down our left flank. They gave their lives, we cannot let them slip into purgatory.

VAN HELSING
So you're sending me into hell.

CARDINAL JINETTE
In a manner.

An old Muslim Cleric steps up and hands something to the Cardinal. The Cardinal holds it up for Van Helsing. It's a TORN PIECE OF PAINTED CLOTH encased in a strip of glass.

CARDINAL JINETTE (cont'd)
The old knight left this here four hundred years ago. We don't know its purpose, but he would not have left it lightly.

Van Helsing stares at it. Painted on the cloth is PART OF A LATIN INSCRIPTION.

CARDINAL JINETTE (cont'd)
In Latin inscription translates as: "In the name of God, open this door."

And then a look of confusion washes over Van Helsing's face. In the corner of the cloth is an INSIGNIA in the shape of a DRAGON. Van Helsing holds his hand up next to the insignia. *On Van Helsing's hand is a RING with the exact same DRAGON INSIGNIA.* The

Cardinal sets his hand on Van Helsing's arm, fatherly.

CARDINAL JINETTE (cont'd)
I think that in Transylvania, you may find the answer you seek. . . .

On Van Helsing's look WE CUT TO:

INT. ARMORY – DAY
Van Helsing strides through a huge blast of steam. An extremely earnest little Friar scurries up, this is CARL.

CARL
There you are. Did you bring him back? Or did you kill him?

Van Helsing doesn't even slow down. Carl shakes his head.

CARL (cont'd)
You killed him, didn't you? That's why they get so annoyed. When they ask you to bring someone back, they don't mean as a corpse.

Van Helsing scowls under his breath. Carl smiles.

CARL (cont'd)
Ah! Right. You're in a mood. Well, come on, I've got a few things that will put the bit back in your mouth.

Van Helsing is suddenly attracted to some swords coming out of a flaming forge. Carl grabs him and pulls him away.

CARL (cont'd)
Any idiot can make a sword.

A huge, beefy, Buddhist Monk covered in sweat steps out from behind the forge, staring daggers at Carl.

CARL (cont'd)
Sorry, father!

Carl grabs some items off a shelf and stuffs them into Van Helsing's arms:

CARL (cont'd)
Rings of garlic, holy water, a wooden stake, a silver crucifix . . .

Van Helsing watches some Spanish priests fire a Gatling gun.

VAN HELSING
Why can't I use one of those?

Carl looks at Van Helsing like he's talking to a child.

CARL
You've never gone after vampires before have you?

VAN HELSING
Vampires, gargoyles, warlocks, they're all the same, best when cooked well.

CARL
They are not all the same. A vampire is nothing like a warlock. My granny could kill a warlock.

VAN HELSING
Carl, you've never even been out of the abbey, how do you know about vampires?

CARL
That's why they make books.

He gestures to a collection of manuscripts by Socrates, Copernicus, Da Vinci, and Galileo, then steps up to a glass OVEN where sticks of dynamite are dripping sweat into vials.

CARL *(cont'd)*
Here's something new. Glycerine 48.

Carl sticks his pinky into a vial and then flicks a drop of the dynamite sweat against a wall, the drop bursts into a large ball of flame. Several of the startled clergy YELL OUT:

SEVERAL PRIESTS
Knock it off, Carl!

CARL
Sorry! Sorry!
(aside to Van Helsing)
The air around here is thick with envy.

Carl grabs a strange-looking CROSSBOW and hands it to Van Helsing, it's covered in little iron pumps and copper tubes.

CARL *(cont'd)*
This is my latest invention.

VAN HELSING
Now this I like.

CARL
Gas propelled, capable of catapulting bolts in rapid succession at tremendous velocity. Just pull the trigger and hold on.
(he adjusts the sight)
I've heard the stories coming out of Transylvania, trust me, you'll need this. A work of certifiable genius.

VAN HELSING
If you don't say so yourself.

Carl doesn't get sarcasm.

CARL
I did say so myself.
(earnest, not bragging)
I am a veritable cornucopia of talent.

Van Helsing picks up a very odd-looking CONTRAPTION.

VAN HELSING
Did you invent this?

CARL
I've been working on that for twelve years. It's compressed magma from Mount Vesuvius with pure alkaline from the Gobi Desert. It's one of a kind.

VAN HELSING
What's it for?

CARL
I have no idea, but I'm sure it will come in handy.

Carl scurries on as Van Helsing follows.

VAN HELSING
Twelve years and you don't know what it does?

CARL
I didn't say that. I said I don't know what it's for. What it does is create a light equal to the intensity of the sun.

VAN HELSING
And this will come in handy how?

Carl hefts two huge duffle bags filled with weaponry into Van Helsing's arms.

CARL
I don't know. You could blind your enemies. Charbroil a herd of charging wildebeest. Use your imagination.

VAN HELSING
No, Carl, I'm going to use yours, that's why you're coming with me.

CARL
The hell be damned if I am.

VAN HELSING
(points an accusing finger)
You cursed. Not very well, but you're a monk, you're not supposed to curse at all.

CARL
Actually, I'm still just a friar, I can curse all I want . . . damn it.

VAN HELSING
The Cardinal has ordered you to keep me alive . . .

He shoves the huge duffle bags into Carl's arms.

VAN HELSING *(cont'd)*
. . . for as long as possible.

Van Helsing turns and heads off through the flaming forges. Carl, carrying the huge duffle bags, staggers off after him.

CARL
But I'm not a field man!

A blast of STEAM fills FRAME, and then the CAMERA is suddenly flying through CLOUDS. . . .

EXT. TRANSYLVANIA – GLOOMY DAY
The CAMERA rips out of the clouds and dives down between two craggy mountain peaks, revealing the strange village of VASERIA nestled in the heart of a creepy valley. The CAMERA whips down into the village and crests the rooftops, as it

lands next to a chimney, three WHITE WINGS drop down around it and TRANSFORM into familiar gowns. The CAMERA holds on the village square below, bustling with activity. Aleera trembles with anticipation.

ALEERA
(Romanian – subtitled)
I am very, very excited about this.

Marishka pouts.

MARISHKA
(Romanian – subtitled)
Why can't we just let the Werewolf kill her?

Verona gives her a condescending look.

VERONA
Never trust a man to do a woman's job.

EXT. VILLAGE SQUARE – DAY
Wearing hoods, heads down, Van Helsing and Carl move through the vicious-looking crowd. Carl whispering to Van Helsing.

CARL
. . . so you can remember everything about your life from the last seven years, but nothing before that?

VAN HELSING
Not now, Carl.

Van Helsing's keen eyes are busy casing the locals.

CARL
There must be something?

VAN HELSING
(dead serious)
I remember fighting the Romans at Masada.

CARL
That was in 73 A.D.?

VAN HELSING
You asked.

Carl suddenly notices what Van Helsing has already taken in, the villagers have been sneaking suspicious glances at them.

CARL
What are we doing here? Why is it so important to kill this Dracula anyway?

VAN HELSING
Because he's the son of the devil.

CARL
I mean besides that.

VAN HELSING
Because if we kill him, anything bitten by him or created by him will also die.

CARL
I mean besides that.

Van Helsing gives him a look. Top Hat steps up to them.

TOP HAT
Welcome to Transylvania.

All the villagers suddenly have knives, machetes, and pitchforks in their hands, and they're all staring at Van Helsing and Carl. Carl nervously whispers to Van Helsing.

CARL
Is it always like this?

VAN HELSING
Pretty much.

A pair of RIDING BOOTS step up onto the well in front of them. It's Anna, she gestures to the two men.

ANNA
You! Let me see your faces.

Under the hat, we see Van Helsing's eyes taking her in.

VAN HELSING
Why?

ANNA
Because we don't trust strangers.

VAN HELSING
I don't trust anyone.

Top Hat pulls out a measuring tape and starts measuring Carl.

TOP HAT
Strangers never last long here.

ANNA
Gentlemen, you will now be disarmed.

Several village men move forward. Van Helsing glares at them.

VAN HELSING
You can try.

The men stop in their tracks, their resolve wavering in his glare.

ANNA
You refuse to obey our laws?

VAN HELSING
The laws of men mean little to me.

ANNA
Fine.
(she looks out at the crowd)
Kill them.

All the villagers raise their weapons and start to close in.

VAN HELSING
I'm here to help you.

ANNA
I don't need any help.

VAN HELSING
Really?

Van Helsing whips the crossbow out from behind his back, the bow snaps out, aimed right at Anna. Anna reacts and ducks, *REVEALING the three brides flying in formation right behind her, coming right at her.*

The brides are now HUGE, WHITE, VICIOUS BATS FROM HELL, we know it's the brides because their faces are still very distinct within the composition of the creatures.

Van Helsing fires. Three bolts. The brides split up as the bolts whiz past, just missing them. The white spectres swoop up over the rooftops and around the Byzantine church spire.

VILLAGERS
Nosferatu!!

All hell breaks loose. The bats rocket around the square, ripping doors and shutters off their hinges, blowing tables and chairs end-over-end, throwing people ass-over-teacups.

ANNA
Everybody inside!

Van Helsing keeps firing, trying to get a bead on them. Aleera swoops down, heading for Anna. Anna sees her coming and leaps off the well, right onto Van Helsing, they crash to the ground. Van Helsing looks at Anna sprawled across him.

VAN HELSING
Normally, I don't like women who throw themselves at me. . . .

Anna is suddenly ripped up off of him by Marishka. Van Helsing bounds up onto the well, leaps out and grabs Anna.

VAN HELSING (cont'd)
Thought you said you didn't need any help.

The two of them drop free and hit the ground. Anna lands on Van Helsing, her thighs straddling his face. He grabs her and rolls her to the ground.

VAN HELSING (cont'd)
Stay here.

She grabs *him* and rolls *him* to the ground.

ANNA
You stay here. They're trying to kill me.

Anna instantly leaps up and runs. Van Helsing gets up to go after her, then spots his crossbow through the trampling crowd. Verona and Marishka fly up over the rooftops.

VERONA
Marishka, my dear, please kill the stranger.

MARISHKA
Love to.

Van Helsing grabs his crossbow and spins around to see Aleera and Verona flying through the chaos, tossing peasants out of their way, chasing Anna. Van Helsing dashes across the square, he fires again, sending Aleera scattering.

VAN HELSING
Carl! I'm out!

Carl races forward, pulls out a clip and throws it to Van Helsing. Van Helsing catches it just as Marishka swoops in on him. Van Helsing dives to the ground in the nick of time. Marishka's clawed feet end up grabbing a cow, she lifts it into the air and pitches it through a second-story balcony.

Van Helsing leaps up, slams the clip home and spins to see Anna racing across the far side of the square, Verona still on her tail. Van Helsing shoulders the crossbow and fires, multiple bolts, rapid fire, tremendous velocity. Dozens of arrows rip into the storefronts all around Verona *and Anna*. Anna leaps over some crates as Verona swoops over her, just missing her. Verona grabs a running man and lifts him up into the air. The man screams in horror. Verona just smiles.

VERONA
Be happy in the knowledge that your blood shall keep me beautiful.

Verona bites into his neck. Top Hat cackles at this from behind a rack of coffins. Anna leaps up from behind the crates, dozens of arrows are imbedded everywhere. Anna gives Van Helsing an angry look.

ANNA
Who are you trying to kill?!

The whole square suddenly goes dead quiet. The brides are nowhere in sight. All the villagers are hunkered down, looking around. Van Helsing gives Anna a questioning look. She nods upwards.

ANNA (cont'd)
The sun.

Van Helsing sees a sliver of SUN shining through the clouds. Then he hears a loud SPLASH. He and Anna turn and look at the well. They move in on it, weapons drawn. They peer into the well. Above them, *the clouds cover the sun.* Carl reacts.

CARL
Van Helsing!

Too late. Aleera rockets up out of the well. Van Helsing is blown back as Aleera grabs Anna and flies up into the air. Van Helsing leaps up and aims, but he can't get a clear shot.

Anna's boots skim the rooftops. She reaches down with her free hand, withdraws a SWITCHBLADE from an ankle strap, flicks it open and slashes Aleera's ankle. Aleera SHRIEKS with a mouth filled with fangs, then throws Anna into the air. Verona swoops in and grabs her. The blade goes flying.

Van Helsing tracks the huge bat with his crossbow, then fires a single shot. The lone arrow impales Verona's foot, she SHRIEKS in pain and rage. Anna drops free, falls onto a rooftop and tumbles down. She manages to grab a gutter forty feet up and dangle precariously. She leaps off the roof, flips through the air, lands upside down on the side of a tree, then jumps the rest of the way to the ground and runs like hell. And that's when Carl sees something.

CARL (cont'd)
Van Helsing! Two o'clock!

Van Helsing pivots in time to see Marishka coming right at him. He fires. A half dozen bolts peg into Marishka. She spirals wildly across the square and crashes straight through the side of a building.

INT. VILLAGE HOME – DAY
Anna sprints into a house, slams the door shut, bolts it tight and turns to go. Aleera's face is right in front of her, dangling upside down from a ceiling beam, she licks her bleeding ankle and smiles coquettishly.

ALEERA
Do you know how long I have wanted to kill you?

Anna is clearly afraid, but trying to hide it as she slowly backs away.

ANNA
Aleera, did I do something to you in a past life?

Aleera flips off the beam and lands between Anna and the door. Anna backs away into the living room as Aleera closes in for the kill.

ALEERA
Don't play coy with me, Princess, you're just like all the other pretty little ancestors in your family. Saying you want to destroy my master, but I know what lurks in your lusting heart.

ANNA
I hope you have a heart, Aleera, because someday I'm going to drive a stake through it.

Aleera throws a casual UPPERCUT, launching Anna like a rag-doll through a closed window.

EXT. ALLEY – DAY
Anna crashes through the shattering window, lands catlike on the ground, and launches herself down an adjacent alley.

EXT. SQUARE – DAY
Van Helsing and Carl creep towards the building that Marishka crashed though. From inside they can hear sobbing.

MARISHKA (O.S.)
My face, look what you've done to my face . . .

Van Helsing slowly moves towards the building, crossbow shouldered. The front door suddenly blows open. Marishka blasts out and BACKHANDS Van Helsing fifty feet through the air. His crossbow goes flying.

Marishka wings around the square, arrows imbedded in her chest and face. Carl dives out of her way as she rips the arrows out, one by one, then lands on a balcony and TRANSFORMS back into a beautiful girl. Van Helsing rolls over in time to see Marishka's wounds COMPLETELY HEAL. Carl leaps up.

CARL
This should do the trick!

Van Helsing looks at him. Carl throws a familiar steel and glass bottle.

CARL (cont'd)
Holy water!

The bottle flips through the air, Verona suddenly swoops in and snatches it. She throws it into the well and looks at Marishka.

VERONA
Finish him.

Then she flies off. Marishka looks at Van Helsing and smiles.

MARISHKA
Too bad. So sad.

Van Helsing looks over at THE CHURCH. WE CRASH ZOOM across the square to a TIGHT SHOT of a basin of Holy Water. Then WE WHIP PAN onto Marishka, she looks from the Holy Water to Van Helsing. His eyes. Her eyes. Both of them are gearing up.

INT. PUB – DAY
Anna careens into a pub and skids to a stop. Aleera is casually sipping a glass of very red wine. A man lies dead across the bar next to her. Anna spins around, but Verona is now right behind her.

VERONA
Hello, Anna, my dear.

She starts to move in for the kill. Anna stumbles back into a wall, cornered.

ANNA
You won't have me, Verona.

Verona just smiles pleasantly and licks her lips.

VERONA
The last of the Valerious.

EXT. VILLAGE SQUARE – DAY
Van Helsing looks at his crossbow, half way between him and Marishka. Marishka leaps up onto the balcony railing, her arms out, ready to take flight, daring him to make the first move. Van Helsing goes for

it. Racing for the crossbow. Marishka leaps out and TRANSFORMS into a huge bat. Van Helsing dives and rolls as Marishka swoops over him. Van Helsing leaps up with his crossbow.

EXT. PUB DAY
Verona opens her mouth, her canines distend into horrible fangs. Anna throws a punch. Verona grabs her hand, lightning quick, and forces Anna to her knees. Aleera steps up.

ALEERA
I want first bite.

Verona nods her consent. Aleera bends down for the kill.

EXT. VILLAGE SQUARE – DAY
Van Helsing runs like hell for the church. Marishka plunges down into the square, laughing wildly. Van Helsing makes it to the basin and slams the tips of his arrows into the water. Marishka rockets right at his back, claws and fangs extended. Van Helsing spins and FIRES. Bolts from the crossbow strafe into the rocketing bat, only this time Marishka SHRIEKS horribly, accompanied by the sound of sizzling flesh. She spirals up and SLAMS into the middle of the church spire.

INT. PUB – DAY
Verona and Aleera both SCREAM. Anna is blown across the pub by a shock wave of wind as the *brides become bats*.

EXT. VILLAGE SQUARE – DAY
Van Helsing pivots as the two spectres crash up through a rooftop and fly into the air, he aims to fire, but they quickly fly off, WAILING insanely. Van Helsing steps back from the church and looks up.

The dying bat is pinned to the spire by the arrows in it's chest. The crowd goes quiet, staring up as the hellish thing slowly TRANSFORMS back into a gorgeous young girl. Marishka glares down at Van Helsing and hisses, then DECAYS into molten rot, shrieking all the way.

Carl looks over and notices the cow, standing on the second floor balcony, looking confused.

As the villagers crawl out from under all the wreckage, some of them start pointing accusing fingers at Van Helsing

VILLAGERS
He killed a bride. He killed Marishka! He killed a vampire!

Now Carl is confused.

CARL
Isn't that a good thing?

Top Hat steps up with an amused smile.

TOP HAT
The vampires only kill what they need to survive, one or two people a month. Now they will kill for revenge.

The angry villagers move in with their pitchforks and machetes. Carl looks back at Van Helsing.

CARL
Are you always this popular?

VAN HELSING
Pretty much.

Top Hat smiles politely and tips his hat at Van Helsing.

TOP HAT
And what name, my good sir, do I put on your gravestone?

And that's when Anna steps up.

ANNA
His name is Van Helsing.

A MURMUR washes over the Transylvanian crowd, but unlike with the French, it is in *admiration*, not fear.

VILLAGERS
Van Helsing . . . It's Van Helsing . . .

Anna gives Van Helsing a nod.

ANNA
Your reputation precedes you.

Van Helsing gives her a hard look back.

VAN HELSING
Next time, stay close, you're no good to me dead.

Anna is momentarily ruffled by this, then she laughs.

ANNA
Well, I'll say this for you, you've got courage.
(she turns to the crowd)
He's the first one to kill a vampire in over a hundred years!

She gives the handsome rogue an appraising look.

ANNA (cont'd)
I'd say that's earned him a drink.

INT. CASTLE DRACULA TOWER – NIGHT
TIGHT ON a DRAGON INSIGNIA, like the one on Van Helsing's ring. Carved into an open COFFIN covered in snow and ice. The snow and ice suddenly melt into STEAM as Dracula rises up out of it.

DRACULA
MARISHKAAA—!!

We are deep in the bowels of a thirteenth-century fortress. It's like nothing we've ever seen before. Everything is covered in a thick permafrost. Great icicles hang down from the ceiling. Icy stalagmites rise up from the floor.

With weird, feral movements, Dracula jerks himself out of his coffin and walks up an enormous pillar. As he passes ancient candelabras, the candles mysteriously ignite.

DRACULA (cont'd)
If it's not the Christians, it's the Moors! Why can't they just leave us alone. We never kill more than our fill. And less than our share. Can they say the same?

Dracula walks UPSIDE DOWN across the forty-foot-high ceiling.

DRACULA (cont'd)
Did I not say how important it was to finish with these Valerious.

He comes face-to-face with Verona and Aleera, hanging from a beam by their feet, cradled in each others arms, sobbing.

DRACULA (cont'd)
Now that we are so very close to fulfilling our dream?

The brides wail in anguish, Dracula's demeanor changes on a dime, from anger to sympathy.

DRACULA (cont'd)
There, there, my lovelies. Do not worry, I shall find another bride.

The brides are appalled.

ALEERA
Do we mean so little to you!?

VERONA
Have you no heart!

DRACULA
No! I have no heart. I feel no love. Nor fear, nor joy, nor sorrow. I am hollow! Soulless! At war with the world and every living soul in it! . . . But soon . . . very soon, the final battle will begin.

His demeanor changes on a dime again, he smiles curiously.

DRACULA (cont'd)
I must find out who our new visitor is.

Dracula jumps the forty feet to the ground with ease. The huge SHADOW of a Werewolf prowls across the wall behind him, a chain around its neck. Dracula smiles at it.

DRACULA (cont'd)
We'll have to make a special aperitif out of him. We are much too close to success to be interrupted now.

Both brides immediately panic and leap off their perch, drop the forty feet and land next to Dracula.

ALEERA
No, my lord! Please! Say you won't try again!

VERONA
My heart could not bear the sorrow if we fail again.

DRACULA
SILENCE—!!

The brides cower in fear. Dracula is immediately horrified, as if he hurt a little child, he envelops them in his cape.

DRACULA (cont'd)
No, no, no. Do not fear me, you must not fear me, everyone else fears me.

The brides calm down and begin to purr in his grasp.

DRACULA (cont'd)
But we must try . . . we have no choice but to try. . . . For our own survival.

Dracula inhales, smelling his brides, but his reverie is broken by the roar of the Werewolf. Behind them, the werewolf's shadow is being poked by a long stick held by a HUNCHBACK'S SHADOW, the poking is accompanied by the sound of electric shocks.

DRACULA (cont'd)
Igor!

The creepy hunchback himself scurries up, slipping across the ice, carrying a ten-foot-long electric cattle prod.

IGOR
Yes, Master!

DRACULA
Why do you torment that thing so?

IGOR
It's what I do.

DRACULA
Remember Igor, "Do unto others."

IGOR
Yes, Master, before they do unto me.

DRACULA
Now go.

Dracula looks up into the rafters.

DRACULA (cont'd)
All of you!

A large gang of vile little DWERGI are perched along the beams. German Gothic trolls, short and squat, with weird masks and goggles that completely hide their faces.

DRACULA (cont'd)
To Castle Frankenstein!

INT. VALERIOUS MANOR ARMORY – NIGHT
A huge door is thrown open, revealing the

Valerious ARMORY. Four centuries' worth of nasty weaponry in cases and racks. Anna charges in, a woman on a mission.

ANNA
So how did you get here?

CARL
We came across the Sea.

ANNA
Really? The sea? The Adriatic Sea?

Van Helsing is all business.

VAN HELSING
Where do I find Dracula?

ANNA
He used to live in this very house, four centuries ago, no one knows where he lives now.

She gestures to a huge oil PAINTING covering an entire wall, a rich and fantastical MAP OF TRANSYLVANIA.

ANNA (cont'd)
My father would stare at that for hours looking for Dracula's lair.

Anna grabs a sword, an iron mace, and some throwing stars.

ANNA (cont'd)
So that's why you've come?

VAN HELSING
I can help you.

ANNA
No one can help me.

VAN HELSING
I can try.

ANNA
You can die trying. All of my family has. I can handle this myself.

VAN HELSING (wry sarcasm)
So I noticed.

Anna spins on him, angry.

ANNA
The vampires attacked in daylight, they never do that. I was unprepared. It won't happen again.

VAN HELSING
Why did they attack in daylight?

ANNA
Clearly they wanted to catch me off guard. They seem almost desperate to finish off my family.

VAN HELSING
Why is that? Why now?

ANNA
You ask a lot of questions.

VAN HELSING
Usually I ask only two, what are we dealing with, and how do I kill it?

Anna straps on a metal chest plate and spiked gauntlets.

ANNA
My father spent most of his life looking for answers, year after year,
(gestures out the window)
tearing apart that tower, combing through the family archives.

On that, Van Helsing looks at Carl, admiring the weaponry.

VAN HELSING
The tower. Start there.

CARL
Right.

Van Helsing keeps staring at Carl. Carl looks confused.

CARL (cont'd)
Now?

Van Helsing doesn't even bother to respond. Carl quickly heads out.

CARL (cont'd)
Right. The tower. Now.

Anna grabs a scabbard, straps it on and heads for the swords. Van Helsing blocks her path.

VAN HELSING
The only way to save your family is to stay alive until Dracula is killed.

ANNA
And who will kill him if not me? Who will show courage, if not me?

VAN HELSING
If you go out there alone, you'll be out-manned and out-positioned.
(gestures out a dark window)
And you can't see in the dark.

Anna laughs this off and moves forward. Van Helsing closes the gap between them, inches from her eyes.

VAN HELSING (cont'd)
In the morning, we'll hunt him together.

Anna stares up into his dark eyes.

ANNA
Some say you're a murderer, Mister Van Helsing, others say you're a holy man, which is it?

VAN HELSING
A bit of both, I think.

A slight smile creases Anna's beautiful face.

ANNA
I promised you a drink. The bar is down the hall, help yourself. As for me . . .
(her eyes go dark)
I'm going.

Anna grabs a sword and slams it into her scabbard. Van Helsing watches her.

VAN HELSING
I'm sorry you have to carry this burden.

ANNA
On the contrary, I would wish for it no other way.

And she means it. She grabs a vicious-looking helmet, black-on-black with sharp metal flanges. Van Helsing stares at her, his respect for her growing.

VAN HELSING
And I'm sorry about your father and brother.

ANNA
I will see them again.

She turns to Van Helsing, her convictions rock solid.

ANNA *(cont'd)*
We Transylvanians always look on the brighter side of death.

VAN HELSING
There's a brighter side of death?

ANNA
Yes, it's just harder to see.

She slams her helmet on and starts to charge out. Van Helsing grabs her arm, spins her around and blows a blue powder into her face. Anna falls back into a wall, out cold. Van Helsing grabs her in his arms before she falls to the floor.

VAN HELSING
I'm sorry about that too.

EXT. MANOR VALERIOUS – RAINY NIGHT
Manor Valerious spikes up into the dark sky, where menacing clouds roil across a FULL MOON. The MUSIC tells us we're building to something very scary.

INT. ANNA'S BEDROOM – NIGHT
Anna is waking up on her bed, her clothes are on, but her armor and weapons have been removed. She suddenly sits up and CURSES in ROMANIAN, then leaps out of bed.

ANNA
Oh my god that hurts . . .
(then she gets angry)
That son-of-a-bitch.

She leaps out of bed and storms for the door.

EXT. GRAND HALLWAY – NIGHT
Except for the RAIN splattering against the windows and the ominous music, it's quiet, very quiet, as Anna storms down the hall. Suddenly, something CREAKS. Anna

freezes. The sound came from behind a door. Anna opens it and enters.

INT. VALERIOUS ARMORY – NIGHT
Anna steps into the armory and angrily looks into the dark.

ANNA
Van Helsing!?

Another CREAK. Coming from somewhere in the cases. Anna is suddenly on the alert, her eyes scan the gloom. She grabs a lantern out of a sconce and moves into the racks. Another CREAK. Anna stops and cocks the lantern back, whoever it is, she's going to let them have it. Then she moves on, and then slowly peaks around a corner. It's just an open window, the wind and rain forcing the shutter to creak against the wall.

Anna breathes a sigh of relief. Steps over and closes the window, the FULL MOON glows outside. And then she sees WET PAW PRINTS on the floor, her breath hitches. Her eyes follow the paw prints, which vanish out in the middle of the floor.

HIGH ANGLE POV: A single eerie musical note signals the presence of something evil, looking down on Anna. Anna instantly knows she's in trouble, starts backing away, breathing harder, she grabs a spiked mace. The POV slowly glides across the ceiling, following her.

Anna feels the presence, but she doesn't know where it's coming from, she spins around. Nothing's there. She moves on, quicker now, weaving through the cases of weaponry. Then she hears a LOW GROWL and freezes, trapped in the middle of the armory, she cocks her arm back. A long terrifying beat.

And then a single drop of rain drops down onto her cheek.

Anna looks straight up. It's a Werewolf. Fangs. Claws. Fur. Dripping wet. Dangling from a beam above her, staring down. It ROARS. Anna runs like hell, past a window. WE HOLD on the window to see dark clouds completely cover the full moon.

Anna rounds a corner and slams into someone. She screams and starts to swing the mace. VELKAN grabs her arm. Anna is shocked.

ANNA *(cont'd)*
Velkan! Oh my God! You're alive!

VELKAN
Quiet, Anna, I only have a moment.

ANNA
But Velkan, there's a Werewolf!

VELKAN
Never mind that! Listen to me! I know Dracula's secret! He has mumblich nowger lochen . . .

Velkan has lost control of his mouth. And that's when Anna notices that his clothes are torn to shreds. Anna recoils. Velkan's body starts to spasm and jerk, he lurches STRAIGHT UP THE WALL. He desperately forces his head to turn and look out a window.

The roiling clouds suddenly clear and reveal the full moon.

VELKAN (cont'd)
Anna! RUN!

But Anna is frozen in place, staring at her brother, ten feet up the wall, who now TRANSFORMS into a Werewolf. The front door bursts open. Van Helsing charges in. Guns drawn.

VAN HELSING
Anna!?

The Werewolf looks out over the cases, sees Van Helsing enter the room. The Werewolf throws itself through the balcony doors. Shattered glass and rain scatter around Anna as Van Helsing runs up.

VAN HELSING (cont'd)
Are you alright?

She's too shocked to answer. He races out onto the balcony and looks down.

EXT. MANOR VALERIOUS – NIGHT
The Werewolf scampers horizontally across the side of the manor. It leaps off, splashes down into the river and heads into the village.

INT. VALERIOUS ARMORY – NIGHT
The armory door crashes open. Van Helsing spins back into the room. It's Carl. He sniffs the air.

CARL
Why does it smell like wet dog in here?

Van Helsing holsters his revolvers and strides for the door.

VAN HELSING
Werewolf.

CARL
Ah! Right. You'll be needing silver bullets then.

Carl scrounges around in his frock and pulls out a bandolier filled with gleaming SILVER BULLETS. He tosses it to Van Helsing, who catches it and slings it over his shoulder. Anna snaps out of her shock and runs after Van Helsing.

ANNA
No. Wait!

Van Helsing slams the door shut behind him. We hear something slam onto the opposite side. Anna runs up and struggles with the door, but it's jammed tight. She is not a happy camper.

ANNA (cont'd)
Van Helsing!

EXT. STREETS – NIGHT
Van Helsing quietly stalks the labyrinthine streets of the village, chambering rounds of silver bullets, on the hunt. The only sound is the muffled revelry coming from pubs.

Van Helsing suddenly senses something and spins around, guns up, scans the darkness, inhales deeply, then smiles.

VAN HELSING
Wet dog.

A FLASH OF FUR suddenly explodes out of a distant alley, and then in a blur of incredible speed, dodges back and forth across the street, from doorway to doorway, getting closer and closer, always hidden or one step ahead of Van Helsing's gun barrels. It vanishes into an alley twenty feet in front of him. Van Helsing starts to back away.

VAN HELSING (cont'd)
Who's hunting who?

EXT. GRAVEYARD – NIGHT
Van Helsing spins around a corner and slams his back up against a wall, waiting to be followed. Once again it's quiet, too quiet. And then something slams into the wall right next to him. Van Helsing whips his gun up into Top Hat's face. The "something" that hit the wall was a coffin. Top Hat smiles down the barrels, then tips his hat.

TOP HAT
Well look at that, a perfect fit, what a coincidence.

He heads into the graveyard.

TOP HAT (cont'd)
I see the wolf man hasn't killed you.

VAN HELSING
Don't worry, he's getting to it.

Van Helsing follows, guns up and ready.

VAN HELSING (cont'd)
You don't seem too worried about him?

TOP HAT
Oh, I'm no threat to him, and I'm the one who cleans up after him.

Top Hat sticks his shovel into a fresh grave.

TOP HAT (cont'd)
If you get my meaning.

VAN HELSING
Little late to be digging graves, isn't it?

TOP HAT
Never too late to dig graves. Never know when you'll need a fresh one.

Van Helsing hears something and turns around, his eyes scan the darkness. Behind him, Top Hat raises his shovel and swings it down at Van Helsing's head. Van Helsing spins around and grabs it just before it smashes into his face. Top Hat is terrified. Van Helsing is furious. Then Top Hat's eyes swivel just a hair. Van Helsing sees it and ducks. The blur of fur is exploding out of the darkness behind him.

Top Hat takes the full impact of the beast and is launched sixty feet down the alley. He's dead even before he and the Werewolf hit the light-post.

Van Helsing whirls around. Sees the dazed Werewolf stagger to it's feet. Van Helsing's guns come up. He has the creature in his sights. He squeezes the triggers.

ANNA (O.S.)
NO!

Anna comes out of nowhere and knocks the guns up. They FIRE. Blasting the light on the light-post. The Werewolf hauls-ass around a corner. Van Helsing charges after it, races around the corner in time to see the Werewolf dart off into the dark forest. Anna runs up beside him. Van Helsing turns, grabs her by the throat, and pins her to a wall, furious.

VAN HELSING
Why?

His grip is so tight she can't breath.

ANNA
You're . . . you're choking me.

He loosens his grip only slightly.

VAN HELSING
Give me a reason not to.

Anna stares at him, the look in his eyes terrifies her, but she still won't reveal what she knows.

ANNA
I can't. . . . If people knew . . .

Van Helsing stares at her, then he lets her go. Anna grabs her throat and sucks air. As his fury abates, Van Helsing looks back at Anna.

VAN HELSING
He's not your brother anymore, Anna.

Anna looks at him, surprised.

ANNA
You knew?

VAN HELSING
I guessed.

ANNA
Before or after I stopped you from shooting him?

VAN HELSING
Before.

Now it's Anna's turn to be furious.

ANNA
And still you tried to kill him?

VAN HELSING
He's a werewolf. He's going to kill people.

ANNA
He can't help it. It's not his fault!

VAN HELSING
I know, but he'll do it anyway.

ANNA
Do you understand forgiveness?

VAN HELSING
I ask for it often.

ANNA
They say Dracula has a cure. If there's a chance I can save my brother, I'm going after it.

She starts to storm off. Van Helsing's arm shoots out and stops her.

VAN HELSING
I need to find Dracula.

ANNA
And I need to find my brother! He gave his life for me! He's the only family I have left!

Anna looks at him, tears in her eyes, heartbroken.

ANNA (cont'd)
I despise Dracula more than you can ever imagine, he has taken every-

thing from me, leaving me alone in this world.

She slumps back against the wall, drained. Van Helsing's face softens, an understanding coming to him.

VAN HELSING
To have memories of those you loved and lost, is perhaps harder than to have no memories at all.

He shakes his head with a sigh, then lowers his arm.

VAN HELSING (cont'd)
All right, let's look for your brother.

EXT. CASTLE FRANKENSTEIN – NIGHT
Strangled by a thick mesh of vines and creepers, Castle Frankenstein has somehow grown even more ominous over the last six months. The sky swirls with dense clouds. Lightning flashes. Thunder cracks. But inside, all is dark and quiet.

INT. LABORATORY – NIGHT
A little, gloved Dwerger HAND slams a huge switch down. The laboratory sparks to life. Brilliant arcs of electricity shoot up and down the walls. The massive dynamos, generators, gears, and fan belts kick in. The Dwergi are feverishly preparing the equipment. A flash of lightning attracts Dracula to the shattered skylight.

DRACULA
Igor!

Igor looks down from the skylight, rain lashing his twisted little body, heavy wind practically blowing him off his feet.

IGOR
Yes, Master?!

DRACULA
Have you finished?

IGOR
Yes, all is done! We're coming down to make the final attachments!

DRACULA
Good.

The Werewolf glides in through a fissure in the granite wall, its eyes fixed on Dracula. Dracula purposefully ignores it.

DRACULA (cont'd)
Werewolves are such a nuisance during their first full moon, so hard to control.

The Werewolf TRANSFORMS back into Velkan, bent over in agony. Dracula strides majestically past him.

DRACULA (cont'd)
I send you on a simple errand, to find out who our new friend is, and you stop for a talk with your sister.

VELKAN
Leave her out of this, Count! She doesn't know your secret, and I am soon to take it to my grave.

Dracula steps up to a filthy iron POD, form-fitted for a very large human body. Inside the pod is a BURNT CORPSE.

DRACULA
Don't wish for death so quickly. I intend for you to be quite useful.

VELKAN
I would rather die than help you.

DRACULA
Don't be boring, everyone who says that dies.

Dracula unfastens the metal straps holding the corpse in.

DRACULA (cont'd)
Besides, tonight, after the final stroke of midnight, you'll have no choice but to obey me.

He rips the corpse out of the pod and throws it down in front of Velkan.

DRACULA (cont'd)
Look familiar?

Velkan stares at it, stricken.

VELKAN
Father.

Dracula grabs Velkan, lifts him up off his feet and slams him into the pod. Igor barks orders at several of the Dwergi and they quickly strap Velkan tight to the pod.

DRACULA
He proved useless. But I'm hoping with Werewolf venom running through your veins, you will be of greater benefit.

Dracula grabs a rusty metal SKULLCAP and slams it down onto Velkan's head. Wires and electrodes spring from the skullcap and attach to the dynamos. Velkan struggles to the last.

VELKAN
I may have failed to kill you, Count, but my sister will not!

EXT. FOREST/CASTLE FRANKENSTEIN – NIGHT
Van Helsing and Anna are trotting their horses down a snowy country lane, eyes scanning the forest and the road.

ANNA
For me, this is all personal, it's about family and honor.

She looks over at Van Helsing, curious.

ANNA (cont'd)
Why do you do it? This job of yours, what do you hope to get out of it?

VAN HELSING
I don't know, maybe some self-realization.

ANNA
What have you got out of it so far?

VAN HELSING (thinks hard)
. . . back pains.

Anna smiles. Van Helsing smiles back. And that's when they both spot something on the ground. They halt their horses, leap off and run to a spot on the road. Anna beats him to it, her hand lifts up a long coarse hair.

ANNA
Werewolves only shed before their first full moon. Before the curse has completely consumed them . . .

They look off into the distance. Castle Frankenstein looms over the countryside lit up by lightning from without and huge arcs of electricity from within. Van Helsing and Anna quickly pull their horses towards a decrepit old barn next to the castle.

ANNA (O.S.) (cont'd)
I don't understand, the man who lived here was killed a year ago along with a hideous creature he created.

VAN HELSING (O.S.)
That's when your father went missing.

ANNA (O.S.)
Just after that.

They strap their horses to a post, then step across the snow and up to the edge of the barn. Lightning flashes as they look out at the castle past the battered front gate to the spectacular arcs of electricity flashing out of the windows.

VAN HELSING
Vampires, werewolves, lightning in winter, this truly is a nightmarish place.

Anna just stares out at the hideous castle.

ANNA
I've never been to the sea.

Van Helsing looks at her, she doesn't return the look, lost in thought, wistful.

ANNA (cont'd)
I'll bet it's beautiful.

Van Helsing feels for her. Anna starts for the front door, Van Helsing grabs her and pulls her back.

VAN HELSING
There are those who go in through the front door . . .

He gestures as a flash of lightning reveals a dozen corpses tangled in the foliage around the front door.

VAN HELSING (cont'd)
. . . and there are those who get to live just a little bit longer.

He pulls her off towards the back of the castle.

INT. GOTHIC FOYER – NIGHT
Van Helsing and Anna creep down a huge Gothic foyer, their boots quietly splash through brackish water covering the floor. Suddenly, at the far end of the hall, something small scurries past. Van Helsing lifts his shotgun tight to his shoulder. Anna nods knowingly.

    ANNA
    Dwerger.

    VAN HELSING
    Dwerger?

    ANNA
    One of Dracula's servants. If you get the chance to kill one, do it, because they'd do worse to you.

    VAN HELSING
    Right.

Another little Dwerger steps into view. Van Helsing lowers his shotgun to hip height. The Dwerger YELLS IN ROMANIAN up to someone above him. Anna turns to Van Helsing, stricken.

    ANNA
    They're using my brother for some sort of experiment.

    VAN HELSING
    Anna.

    ANNA *(desperate)*
    My brother is still battling the sickness within him. There's still hope.

Van Helsing grabs her, hushed:

    VAN HELSING
    Anna! There is no hope for your brother, but we can still protect others by killing Dracula.

She stares at him, filled with fury and desperation and sorrow. Van Helsing's sympathetic eyes pierce into her. Thunder rumbles.

INT. LABORATORY – NIGHT
LIGHTNING FLASHES as the Dwergi move like monkeys around all the equipment. Everything is starting to accelerate. Dynamos CRACKLE. Pulleys WHIRL. Electrical arcs FLASH. Dracula turns a flywheel. The pod with Velkan inside it rises up off the floor, heading for the skylight high above.

INT. FOYER – NIGHT
As Van Helsing and Anna come around a huge stone column their faces fill with disgust. Hanging from the ceiling, rafters, and beams are dozens of gooey white maggot-like COCOONS, about the size of watermelons. DRIPPING SLIME.

    VAN HELSING
    You ever see these before?

Anna shakes her head, revolted.

    ANNA
    What do you think they are?

Van Helsing steps up to one and ponders it.

    VAN HELSING
    Offspring.

    ANNA
    What?

    VAN HELSING
    A man, with three gorgeous women, for four hundreds years?

He looks at Anna and cocks an eyebrow. Anna is shocked, she looks out over the cocoons.

    ANNA
    Vampires are the walking dead, it only makes sense that their children are born dead.

Van Helsing checks out an electric wire sticking into the cocoon, then notices wires sticking out of all the cocoons.

    VAN HELSING
    He must be trying to find a way to bring them to life.

All the wires wend their way up the massive stairs and into the flickering laboratory far above.

    VAN HELSING *(cont'd)*
    I was told Dracula and his Brides only kill one or two people a month.

He snaps open his shotgun and smashes open a box of SHELLS. TIGHT on the box of shells MARKED: SILVER NITRATE.

    VAN HELSING *(cont'd)*
    If they bring all of these things to life . . .

He lets the thought finish itself and starts pumping shells into the shotgun.

INT. LABORATORY – NIGHT
Dracula steps up to a huge vat of neon green liquid, he slams the hatch shut and dogs it tight.

    DRACULA
    Let us begin!

Igor and the Dwergi lower blast shields over their heads, then clamber up the towering scaffolding to various power stations. The weather is getting ferocious. Gusts of RAIN whip down from the shattered skylight, backlit by blinding LIGHTNING and accompanied by explosive THUNDER.

INT. FOYER – NIGHT
Van Helsing's fingers dig into one of the cocoons. He pulls out a handful of the dreadful white goo and flings it to the floor. He goes for another handful.

INT. LABORATORY – NIGHT
Dracula spins around into a CLOSE UP:

    DRACULA
    Throw the switches!

EXT. CASTLE SKYLIGHT – NIGHT
A BOLT OF LIGHTNING STRIKES the conductor above the pod, then courses through Velkan's body. Mercifully, we can't hear him scream because one of the straps covers his mouth. A flash of energy shoots down wires and into the castle.

INT. FOYER – NIGHT
The flash of energy rips down all the electrical wires and starts them jumping like scalded snakes. Van Helsing watches this,

then continues digging a hole in the cocoon, his hand suddenly reveals the repulsive little humanoid face of a PYGMY BAT. It has huge, creepy, lidless eyeballs covered in veins, a hairy pig snout, mottled greenish skin, and a gaping maw filled with rows of tiny, razor-sharp fangs. Even with it's eyes open it's obviously lifeless. Anna looks sickened.

Another flash of energy rips down all the electrical wires. And that's when the creepy little thing SNAPS TO LIFE and HISSES. Anna SCREAMS. Van Helsing palms her mouth and pulls her tight. All the cocoons begin PULSING with some sort of repulsive inner life.

High above, Dracula, Verona, and Aleera stride out of the flickering electrical light show and onto a balcony.

Van Helsing and Anna quickly back off into the darkness. A third flash of energy rips down all the electrical wires. All the cocoons begin QUIVERING WILDLY, shocked into animation.

The pygmy bat revealed by Van Helsing suddenly EXPLODES out of it's cocoon. It darts up into the rafters. More cocoons explode open, spraying walls and pillars with gooey white slime. The putrid little things fly around the foyer. Their CHITTERING becomes deafening. Dracula smiles at his Brides.

DRACULA
They must feed. Show them how.

Dracula shoves Aleera and Verona off the balcony.

DRACULA (cont'd)
And beg the devil that this time they stay alive!

The two Brides drop through the air and then TRANSFORM into giant bat form. They fly and cavort with their offspring. Dracula points out the windows and YELLS to his spawn:

DRACULA (cont'd)
You must feed! To the village! TO THE VILLAGE!

Van Helsing whirls out into the foyer.

VAN HELSING
This is where I come in.

ANNA
No! Wait! You can't!

All the windows in the foyer suddenly SHATTER as the brides and their winged vermin start to fly through them.

And that's when Van Helsing OPENS FIRE. Pumping controlled bursts, the silver nitrate flashing weirdly. Several of the hideous things are hit. They BURST INTO BLACK GOO.

Dracula looks down, insanely furious, all he can see is the silhouette of a man in the foyer far below him. Van Helsing slams his shotgun into a holster strapped across his back.

VAN HELSING
Now that I have your attention.

Needless to say, Dracula goes nuts. He screams in rage and leaps off the eighty-foot-high balcony. Van Helsing sprints hell-bent-for-leather back down the foyer. We don't get to see what Dracula has transformed into, but the sound and fury of his wings is tremendous, creating a huge wind that throws everything around and almost knocks Anna off her feet as she leaps out from behind a stone column and races up the staircase, heading for the laboratory.

INT. TOWER BEDROOM – NIGHT
The Valerious tower bedroom looks like it's been ransacked by a librarian. Ancient artifacts, strange relics, and spiritual texts are arranged symmetrically around a huge CANOPY BED. A flicker of lightning illuminates Carl, wide-eyed as he reads from an elaborately inscribed SACRED LATIN TEXT.

CARL
Well, that's interesting. . . .

And then he hears a horrible CHITTERING. Carl runs to a window and looks out. From this distance, it looks like flying monkeys winging their way over the dark

countryside. Carl stares in horror, then turns and runs out of the room.

INT. CASTLE FRANKENSTEIN FOYER – NIGHT
Back in the foyer, the sound and fury and wind dissipate. Then WE CUT TO Dracula's POV, a creepy blue-ish NIGHT-VISION, scanning the foyer. Van Helsing is nowhere in sight. WE TRACK a huge WINGED SHADOW across a wall, it transforms into the shadow of a man. Dracula steps into FRAME.

DRACULA
I can tell the character of a man by the sound of his heartbeat.

He puts his hand to his ear, we can hear the sound of a HEARTBEAT.

DRACULA (cont'd)
Usually when I approach I can almost dance to the beat. . . . Strange that yours is so steady.

INT. LABORATORY – NIGHT
Anna withdraws her sabre as she creeps into the laboratory. The Dwergi are frantically scurrying about. Igor yells above the cacophony of the machinery and the weather.

IGOR
We're losing power! The human is insufficient! Accelerate the generators! Power the dynamos!

Anna notices the pod high above the shattered skylight. Another bolt of lightning strikes it. One of Velkan's arms suddenly breaks loose from the straps and flails wildly.

ANNA
Velkan.

EXT. TOWN SQUARE – NIGHT
Several men and a comely BARMAID dash out of a pub and join dozens of other peasants into the square, staring up into the storm racked skies at the approaching winged vermin.

BARMAID
Oh my God. What do we do? What do we do?

Carl comes racing around the corner.

CARL
RUUUN!!

He grabs the Barmaid and yanks her out of frame as the hideous creatures flock down into the square. Everybody runs like hell. Some people are ripped up off their feet and carried into the air, others are gang tackled and mauled by the creatures. It's like a scene out of *The Birds*.

INT. FOYER – NIGHT
Dracula stalks through the arches. A phosphorescent match suddenly IGNITES at his feet, he looks down. Van Helsing drops out of a ceiling and STABS a wooden stake deep into his chest. Dracula looks at the wooden stake in his chest, then at Van Helsing, standing in a shaft of light. Dracula gives him a rather pleasant smile.

DRACULA
Hello, Gabriel.

Van Helsing freezes. We've never seen him puzzled before. Dracula calmly grabs the wooden stake in his chest, rips it out and casually discards it.

INT. LABORATORY – NIGHT
Anna creeps across a catwalk, suddenly, she hears the SCREAM of charging Dwergi, one to the left, one to the right. Anna clamps her sword between her teeth and leaps out onto a hanging rope. The two Dwergi leap out after her. All three of them climb. The Dwergi getting closer and closer to Anna. One of them grabs her boot. Anna grabs her sword and lashes down, cutting the rope, both Dwergi plummet down into a vat of boiling green liquid.

Igor and the other Dwergi are too busy to have noticed.

IGOR
We must not lose the Master's progeny!

Anna sockets her sabre and keeps climbing.

EXT. VILLAGE – NIGHT
Flying serenely above the scream-filled village, Verona's hideous fanged mouth smiles adoringly.

VERONA
Feed my lovelies! FEED!

She lifts up a terrified man, dangling from her hand, then chucks him out over the village. A swarm of pygmy bats swoops in like piranha, grabbing him and tearing him apart.

INT. FOYER – NIGHT
A dawning realization washes over Dracula.

DRACULA
You don't remember, do you?

Suspicious, Van Helsing backs off into the ancient foyer.

VAN HELSING
Exactly what should I be remembering?

Dracula follows him, like a cat toying with a trapped mouse.

DRACULA
You are the great Van Helsing. Trained by monks and mullahs from Tibet to Istanbul. Protected by Rome herself! But like me . . .
(his face darkens)
. . . hunted by all others.

VAN HELSING
The Knights of the Holy Order know all about you, so I guess it's no surprise that you would know about me.

DRACULA
Oh, but it's much more than that, you and I go back a long way, Gabriel. I know why you have such horrible nightmares. The horrific scenes of ancient battles past? Do you know how you received those triangular scars on your back?

Van Helsing's eyes narrow, now it's getting really strange.

VAN HELSING
. . . how do you know me?

EXT. CASTLE TOWER – NIGHT
Anna runs up to Velkan, who is still strapped into the pod. She starts unbuckling the belts. Velkan's delirious eyes finally

notice her, a sudden clarity fills them, he starts shaking his head and shoving her away with his free arm.

ANNA
Stop, Velkan! Stop it! It's all right. I've come to save you.

The CLOCK TOWER behind them begins to CHIME MIDNIGHT. Velkan's hand grabs Anna's mouth and starts to grow coarse hair and horrific claws. Anna's eyes practically bug out of her head. She SCREAMS and tries to rip herself away.

INT. FOYER – NIGHT
Van Helsing hears Anna's scream. Dracula just smiles.

DRACULA
So, would you like me to refresh your memory? A few details from your sordid past?

Van Helsing rips a crucifix out of his cloak and thrusts it at Dracula. Dracula SHRIEKS and angrily swats it away, then calms down, smiling beatifically, as if nothing had happened.

DRACULA *(cont'd)*
I guess that's a conversation for another time. But before you go, let me reintroduce myself.
(bows majestically)
Count Vladislaus Dragulia. Born 1432. Murdered 1462.

His bicuspids distend into razor sharp fangs.

EXT. VILLAGE – NIGHT
A third-story window bursts into shards of glass as a woman leaps through it. Two pygmy bats fly out of the window behind her and grab her inches before she hits the pavement.

Carl and the Barmaid come racing around a corner just as the woman is flown up over their heads. Carl lets go of the Barmaid and jumps up to try and save the woman, but she's too high and the hideous vermin carry her off. And that's when Carl hears a scream. He turns and looks.

The Barmaid is clinging to a light post six

feet off the ground, her legs are being yanked up by a pygmy bat. Carl grabs a chair on the run and swings it into the creature. The hideous thing is knocked away. The Barmaid drops into Carl's arms. The creature quickly recovers and charges back for Carl and the Barmaid. The Barmaid screams. Carl screams. The creature suddenly pulls up two feet short of killing them, the look on its hideous face has gone from blood-lust to panic, it frantically claws at its body and then BURSTS INTO MOLTEN FLESH ROT.

HIGH ABOVE THE SQUARE: all of the pygmy bats BURST INTO MOLTEN FLESH ROT. Several people are dropped to their deaths.

The two flying Brides freak out and start to SHRIEK.

INT. FOYER – NIGHT
Dracula spins around at the distant sound of his brides WAILING. Van Helsing uses the moment to leap into a large dumbwaiter and cut the cables with one of his saw blades. Dracula looks back in time to see Van Helsing rocket upwards.

EXT. CASTLE TOWER – NIGHT
The clock CHIMES. Anna SCREAMS. Velkan looks at his hands, eyes widening in horror, he gives his sister one last pathetic look, and then TRANSFORMS into the Werewolf. Anna quickly backs away and slams into another body. She screams and spins around. It's Van Helsing.

> **VAN HELSING**
> I think we've overstayed our welcome.

The fat gun in his hand FIRES. The tether shoots off across the castle moat and slams into the top of a huge oak tree two hundred yards away. Van Helsing quickly ties his end taut.

As the clock CHIMES, the Werewolf sits up in front of it. Viciously tearing his way free, he heads for our two heroes.

Van Helsing scoops Anna up off her feet and leaps over the wall just as the Werewolf rips the shotgun off his back.

Van Helsing and Anna start to rappel down the tether. The Werewolf slashes it, severing it. Van Helsing and Anna are suddenly swinging out over the moat and into the dark forest.

The Werewolf glares after them, filled with an incredible fury as the clock hits the final stroke of midnight. . . .

EXT. VILLAGE – NIGHT
Carl and the Barmaid look around, confused.

> **BARMAID**
> What happened?

> **CARL**
> They . . . they just died.

The Barmaid wraps her arms around Carl and kisses him of the cheek.

> **BARMAID**
> How can I ever repay you?

Carl whispers into her ear. The Barmaid looks shocked.

> **BARMAID** *(cont'd)*
> But you can't do that, you're a monk.

> **CARL**
> Actually, I'm just a friar. . . .

EXT. CASTLE TOWER – NIGHT
High atop the castle tower, Dracula cradles the sobbing brides in his arms. Igor slithers up, looking terrified, if he had a tail, it would be tucked firmly between his legs.

> **IGOR**
> I am sorry, Master. We try and we try, but I fear we are not so smart as Doctor Frankenstein.

Dracula turns to him.

> **DRACULA**
> Truly.

Igor cowers, but Dracula seems spent.

> **DRACULA** *(cont'd)*
> It is clear that the good Doctor took the key to life to his grave.

The Werewolf steps up onto the parapet, an insane look in it's eyes. Dracula waves him away, dismissive.

> **DRACULA** *(cont'd)*
> Hunt them down. Kill them both.

The Werewolf gives him a deranged look and snarls evilly, clearly he is Velkan Valerious no more. He turns and leaps off the parapet.

EXT. MOORS – NIGHT
RAIN lashes down on Van Helsing and Anna as they stagger across the moors, heading into the ruins of the old windmill. With the loss of her brother, Anna doesn't know whether to scream or cry, so she does both, and aims it at Van Helsing.

> **ANNA**
> A wooden stake?! A silver crucifix?! What did you think?! We haven't tried everything before?

Anna shoves Van Helsing back under one of the huge charred windmill sails, a refuge from the rain.

> **ANNA (CONT'D)**
> We've been hunting this creature for more than four hundred years. We've shot him, stabbed him, clubbed him, sprayed him with holy water and staked him in the heart, and still he lives!

Van Helsing just stares at her, fire fascinates him, fiery women even more so. She gets right up into his face.

> **ANNA** *(cont'd)*
> Do you understand? . . . Nobody knows how to kill Dracula.

Their faces are inches apart. RAIN pours down on them. A slight smile creases Van Helsing's lips.

> **VAN HELSING**
> I could've used that information a little earlier.

Anna just scowls, breathing hard. Van Helsing's dark eyes stare at her, he likes being this close to her. But she's too upset.

ANNA
Don't give me that look. I don't need your wolf's eyes undressing me . . .

She shoves herself away and stares off into the rain.

ANNA (cont'd)
. . . not right now anyway.

Van Helsing picks up an undamaged absinthe bottle and admires it. Anna looks at him, the fight going out of her.

ANNA (cont'd)
You were right . . . I'm sorry . . . he isn't my brother anymore.

She steps up closer to him as he uncorks the bottle.

ANNA (cont'd)
Do you have any family, Mister Van Helsing?

VAN HELSING
I'm not sure. I hope to find out some-day, that's what keeps me going.

Anna takes the bottle and holds it up in a toast.

ANNA
Here's to what keeps you going.

She takes a deep slug, clearly it has a bite.

VAN HELSING
Absinthe. Strong stuff.

Anna hands him the bottle.

ANNA
Yes. Don't let it touch your tongue, it'll knock you on your—

—And that's when the soggy ground beneath them suddenly CAVES IN. The two of them and a load of timber drop into a rapidly expanding breach in the ground.

INT. CAVERN – NIGHT
Van Helsing and Anna and a cascade of water and timber crash down into a cavern and WE FADE OUT. . . .

EXT. VILLAGE – DAWN
FADE UP: on the Transylvanian village at dawn.

INT. TOWER BEDROOM – DAY
Carl is asleep on a couch. He suddenly sits up, terrified, then looks down and sees the sleeping Barmaid.

CARL
Ah! Yes . . . now I remember.

Carl leans back against the wall, triggering a secret panel to swing open and reveal a PAINTING: a fantastic mural of two medieval KNIGHTS facing each other atop a sea lashed cliff. There is writing in Latin encircled around the two men. Carl translates it:

CARL (cont'd)
Even a man who is pure in heart, and says his prayers by night, may become a wolf when the wolf-bane blooms, and the moon is shining bright.

He steps up to get a closer look and finish the inscription.

CARL (cont'd)
Or crave another's blood when the sun goes down, and his body takes to flight.

As soon as he finishes the last word, the entire painting COMES ALIVE, trees sway, grass blows, huge waves pound the cliff, the clock on a church tower begins to CHIME, and the two knights TRANS-FORM: one into a Werewolf, the other into a Winged Beast from Hell. They viciously attack each other.

Carl of course freaks out, stumbles back, knocks the entire couch over and lands on the Barmaid's semi-naked body. She angri-ly shoves him off as he looks up at the painting. The ancient painting is back to being just a painting, as if it was all in his mind. He stares at it, perplexed, as his Transylvanian girlfriend angrily gathers her clothes.

BARMAID
Friars, monks, priests, you're all the same!

INT. CAVERN – DAY
Anna slowly wakes up on the dark cavern floor, groggy and sore, she rubs her head and groans. A HAND quickly covers her mouth. She looks up. Van Helsing's finger goes to his lips.

VAN HELSING
Shhh . . . there's something down here.

And it's carnivorous.

He gestures to a massive pile of RAT BONES, picked clean.

Anna gets to her feet. The cavern is lit by a very dim gloom coming from tiny crevices in the roof. A fetid little stream wends its way through the cavern. Van Helsing starts to head downstream. Anna draws her sword and follows.

VAN HELSING (cont'd)
Whatever's down here appears to be of human ancestry.

He gestures to a large set of muddy BOOT PRINTS.

VAN HELSING (cont'd)
I'd say he's a size 17. About 360 pounds. 8 1/2 to 9 feet tall. He has a bad gimp in his right leg. . . . And three copper teeth.

ANNA
How do you know he has copper teeth?

VAN HELSING
Because he's standing right behind you.

Van Helsing goes for his guns. Frankenstein's Monster leaps out of the pitch blackness behind Anna and slams her into Van Helsing. Our two heroes crash to the floor. Van Helsing's revolver goes flying.

The monster is on Van Helsing in a flash, he lifts him up over his head and hurtles him into a rock wall. Van Helsing bounces off the wall and slams to the floor. The monster looks down at Anna. Anna gets a good look at him. He now looks even more horrific than before, having been badly burned so long ago.

ANNA
Oh my god, the Frankenstein monster.

FRANKENSTEIN
MONSTER!?

Frankenstein's VOICE is a horrible, guttural rasp.

FRANKENSTEIN (cont'd)
Who is the monster here?!?

He lifts Anna up off the floor.

FRANKENSTEIN (cont'd)
I have done nothing wrong and yet you and your kind all wish me dead!

Van Helsing leaps up and tackles Frankenstein. Frankenstein's head slams into a rock wall, the top half of his head pops off. Van Helsing grabs him by the neck, the bolts SPARK, Van Helsing is shocked back against the far wall, he crashes to the floor, trying not to pass out from the pain.

Frankenstein slams the top of his head back into place, then the top half of his body turns around and he heads for Anna. Anna backs away, up against some burnt timber, looking around, playing for time.

ANNA
What do you want?

Frankenstein stares down at her, his face growing mournful.

FRANKENSTEIN
To exist.

Van Helsing yanks an ivory BLOWGUN out from inside his cloak and sticks it to his mouth.

Six blow-darts nail Frankenstein in the back. He bellows and spins around, arms flailing at his back, trying to swat the darts free. Anna runs over and picks up one of the revolvers off the ground next to Van Helsing.

ANNA
We must kill it.

Van Helsing grabs her by the wrist.

VAN HELSING
No! Wait.

Frankenstein crashes to his knees, his bleary eyes look over at them.

FRANKENSTEIN
If you value your lives, and the lives of your kind, you will kill me.

Van Helsing pulls Anna behind him and heads for Frankenstein, whose breathing is getting more and more labored.

FRANKENSTEIN (cont'd)
If Dracula finds me . . . I am the key to my father's machine . . . the key to life, life for Dracula's children!

VAN HELSING
He already awakened them, last night.

FRANKENSTEIN
Those were just from one bride, from one single birthing. And they died as they did the last time he tried. Only with me can he give them lasting life.

Van Helsing kneels down beside Frankenstein.

VAN HELSING
There are more? More of those things?

Frankenstein's pathetic eyes stare at him.

FRANKENSTEIN
Thousands . . . thousands more.

Frankenstein passes out, crashing face first into the dirt. WE PUSH IN on Van Helsing as the gravity of this hits him. Anna isn't fazed, she lifts the gun and aims. Van Helsing steps in front of her. She angrily looks him in the eyes.

ANNA
You heard what he said.

Van Helsing holds her stare, searching for the words. . . .

VAN HELSING
My life, my . . . job . . . is to vanquish

evil. I can sense evil.
(gestures to Frankenstein)
This thing . . . man . . . whatever it is, evil may have created it, left its mark on it, but evil does not rule it. So I cannot kill it.

ANNA
I can.

She moves around him. He blocks her path.

VAN HELSING
Not while I'm here.

Anna sees the intensity in his eyes. Behind them, hidden in the shadows, is the Werewolf, staring at Frankenstein.

VAN HELSING (cont'd)
Your family has spent four hundred years trying to kill Dracula, maybe this poor creature can help us find a way.

The Werewolf slowly starts to back away. Van Helsing suddenly senses it and spins around. He and Anna see the Werewolf's shadow vanish down the cavern.

ANNA
Oh my God. He's seen us.
(she turns to Van Helsing)
Now they'll come for him. And neither you or I will be able to stop them.

Van Helsing grabs her arm and heads for Frankenstein.

VAN HELSING
I must get him to Rome. We can protect him there.

On Anna's dubious look WE SMASH CUT TO:

EXT. MANOR VALERIOUS – DAY
STEAM blasts out of the nostrils of huge black horses, covered in a light armor plating, coupled to an ornate COACH. Van Helsing and Carl walk down alongside them.

CARL
. . .and then the painting came alive and the two creatures attacked each other.

VAN HELSING
What does it mean?

CARL
I don't know.

Anna opens the door to the coach. Frankenstein is inside, chained to the back wall. Van Helsing nudges Carl.

VAN HELSING
Whatever you do, don't stare at him.

CARL
I'm staring at him.
(quickly turns away)
Is that a man?

Van Helsing shoves Carl up into the seat across from Frankenstein.

VAN HELSING
Actually it's seven men, parts of them anyway.

Frankenstein struggles to break the chains that bind him.

FRANKENSTEIN
By exposing me, you have condemned me. Me and all of humanity!

Anna slams the door shut and gestures to the horses.

ANNA
Nothing is faster than Transylvanian steeds. Not even a werewolf. Anything else, you're on your own.

COUNTRYSIDE – DAY/NIGHT TRANSITION
On the bottom half of the SCREEN, the coach races across the countryside. On the top half, the sky is whipping past in TIME LAPSE. Dark clouds scream by showing us glimpses of the sun as it races right to left across the SCREEN. As the sun exits FRAME the moon comes up and the TIME LAPSE ends revealing an ominous night sky. The coach races into a dark forest. Two Bride silhouettes fly past and follow it.

EXT. WOODS – NIGHT
The black steeds charge through the woods

pulling the COACH. Van Helsing is in the driver's seat urging them on.

INT. COACH – NIGHT
Frankenstein stomps his Doc Martens and yells out.

FRANKENSTEIN
Free me! Let me fight! Let me die! But do not let me be taken alive!

Sitting across from him is Carl, eyes wide, really keyed up, the blowgun stuck to his lips.

EXT. WOODS – NIGHT
The CAMERA is suddenly hurtling through the misty forest at about Mach 1. The BRIDE'S POV quickly closes in on the coach.

Van Helsing senses them coming, he looks around, the creepy trees sway in the breeze, but he can't see the brides. He hefts the crossbow. He hears something off to his left and looks. And that's when Verona swoops down on his right and grabs him jerking him clean off the driver's seat and up into the air. The crossbow goes flying. Van Helsing quickly breaks free and falls down onto the lead horse. He looks forward.

A hundred yards ahead, the path makes a

hairpin turn next to a giant precipice. Van Helsing quickly looks back at the coach.

INT. COACH – NIGHT
The coach bounces hard. Frankenstein is thrown forward at Carl. Carl screams, but the chains hold Frankenstein just short of falling on him.

FRANKENSTEIN
Let me go.

CARL
Where are you going to go? I don't know if you've looked in the mirror lately, but you kind of stick out in a crowd.

EXT. WOODS – NIGHT
Van Helsing leaps from the front horse to the middle horse to the rear horse and then up onto the buckboard. And that's when Aleera nails him on the fly, throwing him back onto the rear horse.

All of the horses try to make the turn, going full boar, hoofs fighting to avoid slipping over the edge, kicking rocks out into space. Van Helsing holds on for dear life. The coach skids sideways, the couplings SNAP and the coach is flung out over the void.

Van Helsing spins up into a saddle in time

to see the coach spiraling through the air, heading for the valley floor far below.

EXT. IN THE AIR – NIGHT
HIGH UP IN THE AIR: Aleera and Verona freak out.

VERONA
We must not let him be destroyed!

EXT. WOODS – CLIFF FACE – NIGHT
The two Brides fly as fast as they can towards the plummeting coach. They both grab it, but its weight is far too great for them to stop it from falling. Aleera is losing her grip.

ALEERA
Save him! Save the monster!

Aleera is blown off. Verona struggles her way to the door, her wings are being badly buffeted. She grabs the door and rips it off, then looks inside. The coach is empty.

EXT. WOODS – NIGHT
BACK WITH VAN HELSING as ANOTHER COACH races out of the forest and up to the six team. Anna in the driver's seat. Carl leans out the window. Frankenstein is chained inside.

CARL
Come on! Come on!

INT. COACH – NIGHT
BACK INSIDE THE OTHER COACH: Verona sees a bunch of glycerine tubes wrapped around a dozen SILVER SPIKES. Verona hisses in anger and throws herself free of the coach.

EXT. COACH – NIGHT
The coach hits the ground and EXPLODES. Several of the spikes nail Verona in the chest. She shrieks in horror and then TRANSFORMS back into herself. Losing her wings, she drops out of the sky, DECAYING into molten rot, shrieking all the way. Aleera screeches in horror.

EXT. WOODS – NIGHT
Van Helsing leaps from the six team onto the buckboard of the other coach, landing next to Anna. He gives Anna a nudge in the ribs and a cocky smile, as if to say, "I

told you it would work." And that's when 800 pounds of enraged fur leaps over the entire six team, heading right for Van Helsing and Anna.

Van Helsing quickly rolls off one way as Anna flings herself off the other. The Werewolf slams into the buckboard and skids sideways across the roof, shattering all four corner lanterns. The Werewolf vanishes off the back of the coach as the kerosene and the entire roof bursts into flames.

INT. COACH – NIGHT
Carl frantically looks around, then sees Anna's face plastered to the window.

ANNA
CARL!

Carl leaps over and opens the door.

EXT. COACH – NIGHT
Anna is hanging on to the side of the coach, which is now skirting a huge precipice a mile deep. Carl grabs her as she starts to slip.

ON THE OTHER SIDE OF THE COACH: Van Helsing is being violently dragged down the road, desperately clinging by one hand to the axle of the coach. His legs splitting the rear wheel, if he lets go he'll be run over.

VAN HELSING
CARL!

INT. COACH – NIGHT
Carl looks past Frankenstein to the other side of the coach. He can't let go of Anna or she'll fall. He looks at Frankenstein. Frankenstein nods.

FRANKENSTEIN
I can help.

CARL
You won't kill me?

FRANKENSTEIN
Only if you don't hurry.

EXT. COACH – NIGHT
Van Helsing grimaces in pain, his five fin-

gers cling to the axle, then four fingers, then three, two, one. He lets go and heads under the rear wheel. And that's when a huge fist grabs him by the collar and pulls him free. It's Frankenstein. The two men share a look, then Frankenstein heaves Van Helsing upwards. He lands on the buckboard just as Anna swings up next to him.

INT. COACH – NIGHT
Carl looks at Frankenstein and smiles in relief, then he screams bloody murder as he sees FUR moving across the rear window. And then the roof splits open and fire and smoke pours in. Now it's Frankenstein's turn to scream.

EXT. COACH – NIGHT
Van Helsing and Anna look back through the fire towards the rear of the coach. In SLO-MO the Werewolf rises up through the flames.

The side door of the coach smashes open and Frankenstein and Carl look out.

FRANKENSTEIN
Don't look down.

CARL
I'm looking down! I'm looking down!

The coach makes it across the precipice road and enters the forest. The Werewolf hunches. Van Helsing YELLS at Anna.

VAN HELSING
Jump!

Anna turns and leaps off the carriage. So does Carl and Frankenstein. They all vanish into the lush forest.

Van Helsing aims both of his guns down at the coupling and fires. The horses break loose of the carriage. Van Helsing turns and jumps. The Werewolf leaps through the flames.

Van Helsing spins around in mid-air and fires his guns back at the Werewolf just as it tackles him. They vanish into the foliage. The flaming coach flips off the road, spirals through the air and crashes into the trees. The six team hauls-ass down the forest road, vanishing into the night. . . .

EXT. FOREST – NIGHT
Anna staggers through the forest, she rounds a tree, her breath hitches. Lying naked on the ground is her brother. He looks up and gives his sister one last sorrowful look.

VELKAN
Forgive me.

And then he dies. Anna throws herself onto Velkan's body.

ANNA
Velkan! . . . Velkan! . . . Velkan.

She cradles him gently and kisses him on the cheek.

ANNA (cont'd)
I will see you again.

Nearby, Van Helsing staggers to his feet. Anna looks at him, then leaps up and charges him, pummeling him with her fists.

ANNA (cont'd)
You killed him! You killed him!

Van Helsing grabs her by the wrists and holds her tight.

VAN HELSING
Now you know why they call me murderer.

Anna looks into his eyes, they are not angry, but filled with a profound sadness. And then Anna notices BLOOD on his shirt, she gently opens his cloak. Anna gasps. Horrified.

ANNA
Oh my god . . .

Van Helsing's shirt is punctured with bloody fang holes.

ANNA (cont'd)
You've been bitten.

She staggers back and looks at him, she sees it in his eyes. A hint of it anyway. *Fear.* Van Helsing turns and looks down at Velkan's body. Anna turns away. Aleera is standing right there. She backhands Anna.

Anna slams into a tree and drops to the ground, out cold. Van Helsing spins around in time to catch a glimpse of Anna, upside down, being yanked up into the trees. Van Helsing hauls-ass.

EXT. CLIFFSIDE – NIGHT
Van Helsing runs out onto the side of a cliff. He sees Anna being carried off over the precipice by Aleera. Carl and Frankenstein stagger up beside him. All three of them watch the silhouettes of Anna and Aleera flying off towards the lights of a distant city. . . .

EXT. BUDAPEST – DAY
Nestled in a lush valley and split in half by a dark river, the city is sprinkled with churches, mosques, and palaces.

EXT. ALLEY – DAY
Van Helsing, Carl, and Frankenstein stagger down an alley. Battered and bruised. Frankenstein's face is covered by a hood. Van Helsing pulls his cloak tight, keeping his wound hidden. A blast of wind hits them. They all react, Van Helsing flinches in pain as he pulls his gun.

Perched on the snowy eve of a house is Aleera, she clicks her tongue in disapproval.

ALEERA
Tch, tch, tch, so much trouble to my Master, so much trouble.

Frankenstein starts to head for her. Van Helsing stays him. Aleera just giggles.

ALEERA (cont'd)
You killed Verona. If the Master was capable of love, he would have loved her very much. As for me . . .
(she smiles coquettishly)
. . . now I will have the Master's undivided attention.

VAN HELSING
What do you want?

ALEERA
The Master commands a trade. The monster for the Princess.

Frankenstein glares at her angrily, and then he hears Van Helsing's VOICE:

VAN HELSING (O.S.)
Somewhere public. Lots of people.

Frankenstein looks at Van Helsing, feeling betrayed, his brow furrows, his eyes darken. Van Helsing's eyes stay on Aleera.

VAN HELSING (cont'd)
A place where your master will be less inclined to expose his . . . other side.

Aleera chews this over for a moment, then her eyes light up.

ALEERA
Tomorrow night is All Hallow's Eve! Here in Budapest there is a wonderful masquerade ball.

She leaps for joy, all the way up to the top of the roof.

ALEERA (cont'd)
I love masquerade balls!
(she looks down at them)
Vilkova Palace. Midnight.

Then she whoops for joy and leaps again, vanishing over the side of the roof, followed by a blast of wind and snow.

Van Helsing holsters his gun and turns to go, he winces in pain. Carl sees this and reaches for Van Helsing's cloak.

CARL
Are you hurt?

Van Helsing shoves his hand away. Frankenstein's eyes narrow suspiciously, then he lunges forward and rips Van Helsing's cloak open, revealing the puncture wounds in his shirt.

FRANKENSTEIN
He has been bitten! Bitten by a werewolf.

Van Helsing pulls his cloak tight. Frankenstein's face forms a twisted smile.

FRANKENSTEIN (cont'd)
Now you will become that which you have hunted so passionately.

Van Helsing pulls out the BLOWGUN and looks at Frankenstein.

VAN HELSING
I'm sorry.

And he means it. Frankenstein just glares.

FRANKENSTEIN
May others be as passionate in their hunting of you.

Van Helsing FIRES THE DARTS.

EXT. VILKOVA PALACE GRAVEYARD – DUSK
The last shadows of the day stretch like creepy fingers across an ancient ROYAL GRAVEYARD. Wearing costumes and masks, Van Helsing and Carl step out of an old MAUSOLEUM. They shove the huge stone door shut and bar it tight.

CARL
According to the books, you won't turn into a werewolf until the rising of your first full moon, two nights from now, and then you'll still be able to fight Dracula's hold over you until the final stroke of midnight.

The two men make their way through the tombstones, heading for a huge, ornate PALACE next door.

VAN HELSING (sarcastic)
Sounds like I have nothing to worry about.

CARL
Oh my God, you should be terrified.

Van Helsing gives him a look. Then Carl gets it.

CARL (cont'd)
Oh . . . well, um, that still gives us forty-eight hours to find a solution.

Carl looks back at the mausoleum.

CARL (cont'd)
Are you sure he can't get out of there?

VAN HELSING
Not without some help from the dead.

TIGHT on a COFFIN, lying in the frozen ground, waiting to be buried. The lid cracks open, gnarled fingers pry their way out.

INT. BALLROOM – NIGHT
The grand ballroom is packed with dancing couples and alive with JUGGLERS, FIRE BLOWERS, TIGHT ROPE WALKERS, and HIGH WIRE ACROBATS, a veritable Cirque du Soleil. Van Helsing and Carl make their way through all the weirdness.

CARL
Well, this is different.

VAN HELSING
Dracula must have something up his sleeve.

CARL
So in situations like this, do we have a solid plan? Or do we just improvise?

VAN HELSING
A bit of both actually.

They step up to the ornate banquet tables. Van Helsing inhales deeply. Carl does likewise.

CARL
Smells wonderful, doesn't it?

VAN HELSING
Not everything.

CARL
What do you smell?

VAN HELSING
Everything.

Van Helsing looks around, suddenly very suspicious.

VAN HELSING (cont'd)
Warm pretzels, juniper bushes, ladies perfume, and rotted human flesh.

Carl gives him a look.

CARL
You sure do know how to put a damper on the evening.

INT. BALLROOM – NIGHT
OUT ON THE DANCE FLOOR:
Dracula dances with Anna, both wearing masks. He dips her and removes her mask. *She is in a trance.* Eyes open, unblinking. Dracula throws away his mask and kisses her. Anna snaps out of it. Dracula spins her around.

DRACULA
How does it feel to be a puppet on my string?

Anna suddenly looks around, realizing she's dancing with Dracula. She struggles, but is completely within his power.

ANNA
I won't let you trade me, Count.

DRACULA
I have no intention of trading you. And if I know Van Helsing, which I do, he isn't planning on making a trade either.

He dips her and leans in close, their lips almost touching.

DRACULA (cont'd)
Neither of us has ever settled for half.

ANNA
You make my skin crawl.

DRACULA
That's not all I could do with your skin.

Dracula gently caresses her neck. Aleera cuts in and grabs Anna away from Dracula.

ALEERA
My turn.

Aleera dances away with Anna. Dracula smiles, then randomly grabs a passing woman, yanks her close and bites into her neck. The ballroom is in such high swing no one notices.

INT. BALLROOM – SECOND FLOOR – NIGHT
UP ON THE SECOND FLOOR: Van Helsing and Carl look down on the ballroom. Carl spots Aleera dancing with Anna.

CARL
There they are.

VAN HELSING
Something's not right.

CARL
Yes, they're both trying to lead.

VAN HELSING
Not that.

And then Van Helsing spots something, his eyes light up.

VAN HELSING (cont'd)
Carl?

CARL
Yes?

VAN HELSING
I have a plan. I need you to do something.

INT. BALLROOM – NIGHT
BACK ON THE DANCE FLOOR:
Aleera dances Anna across the floor.

ALEERA
It's the little things in life that I love. Like that last look in my victim's eyes just before they die.

We see in Anna's eyes how hard she's struggling to break free. Aleera licks Anna's cheek.

ALEERA (cont'd)
I won't let the Master take you, Anna.

Aleera's canines distend into horrible fangs, the blood draining from her beautiful face.

ALEERA (cont'd)
I want him all to myself.

Anna's eyes widen, helpless in Aleera's grasp. And that's when Dracula cuts in, he gives Aleera a smile.

DRACULA
You look famished, my dear, go get yourself a bite.

Aleera scowls as Dracula spins Anna over to a MIRROR WALL.

DRACULA (cont'd)
Don't we make a beautiful couple?

Anna looks at the mirror. *Dracula is not in the reflection.* He starts to dance with her in front of the mirror.

DRACULA (cont'd)
I'm looking for a new bride, Anna, someone strong and beautiful.

In the mirror it looks like Anna is dancing alone, seemingly being dipped and spun and twirled by an invisible force.

DRACULA (cont'd)
All it takes is one bite from me.

He hugs her tighter. Anna looks from his face to his chest, crushed tightly against her breasts, her eyes widen.

ANNA
You have no heartbeat.

DRACULA
Perhaps it just needs to be rekindled.

Dracula leans in for a kiss. Anna angrily turns her head away, so she doesn't see all the blood drain from Dracula's face and his canines distend into fangs, about to bite into her neck.

A Fire Breather tilts his head safely up and away from the crowd, lifts a torch to his mouth and starts to BLOW. Carl quickly sidles up and shoves him hard. The Fire Breather BLOWS FLAMES across the back of Dracula's cape.

INT. BALLROOM – SECOND FLOOR – NIGHT
UP ON THE BALCONY: Van Helsing dashes down the HIGH WIRE. The TIGHT ROPE WALKERS start to lose their balance.

INT. BALLROOM – DANCE FLOOR – NIGHT
DOWN ON THE DANCE FLOOR:
Dracula whirls around, ON FIRE, shocked and angry.

INT. BALLROOM – ABOVE DANCE FLOOR – NIGHT
HIGH ABOVE THE DANCE FLOOR:

Van Helsing cuts a stay-wire, grabs on and SWINGS DOWN into the crowd. The Tight Rope Walkers ALL FALL.

INT. BALLROOM – DANCE FLOOR – NIGHT
DOWN ON THE DANCE FLOOR:
Dracula grabs the Fire Breather and tosses him clear across the ballroom. Van Helsing swoops in, grabs Anna by her waist and swings her up into the air.

INT. BALLROOM – BALCONY – NIGHT
UP ON THE BALCONY: Van Helsing and Anna land, skid to a stop and look down.

The entire crowd looks up at our heroes. And then, in unison, they all remove their masks. Their eyes go yellow, their skin goes white, fangs glide out, they HISS angrily. They are all VAMPIRES. Dracula smiles up at Van Helsing.

DRACULA
Welcome to my summer palace.

A side door bursts open and a batch of vampires charge in carrying Frankenstein over their heads, he's chained tight and bellowing furiously. Igor stands on his chest.

IGOR
We have him, Master! We have him!

Dracula gives an evil LAUGH, then looks at his followers and gestures to Van Helsing and Anna.

DRACULA
Enjoy yourselves!

The entire vampire crowd rushes forward, SHRIEKING like wild Banshees.

Anna's response is to rip the arm off a SUIT OF ARMOR, stick her hand down the sleeve and into its metal glove, attached to the glove is an IRON MACE covered in spikes. Van Helsing's response is to give her an incredulous look, then grab her and yank her out of FRAME.

INT. BALLROOM HALLWAY – NIGHT
Van Helsing and Anna race down a hallway.

ANNA
Where are we going!?

Van Helsing points to a huge STAINED GLASS WINDOW of angels, cherubs, and saints.

VAN HELSING
Through that window!

ANNA
Are you out of your mind?! We'll be cut to ribbons!

VAN HELSING
Not if you relax when you're going through it.

At the last second Van Helsing notices one of the SAINTS has his hand out, as if to say "STOP." Van Helsing grabs Anna and skids to a stop.

VAN HELSING (cont'd)
My mistake, wrong window.

ANNA
How do you know?

VAN HELSING
Just a hunch.

He yanks her out of FRAME. Vampires bound past, chasing after them. Dracula's LAUGH echoes throughout the palace.

INT. STAIRCASE/HALLWAY – NIGHT
Van Helsing and Anna race up some stairs and through a set of double doors, vampires hot on their tail. They each grab a door, slam it shut and bolt it tight. The vampires furiously smash away from the other side. Van Helsing and Anna high-tail it down the hall.

Carl comes scurrying around a corner at the far end of the hallway. He sees Van Helsing and Anna running towards him and holds up his LAVA CONTRAPTION.

CARL
Now I know what it's for.

Carl is standing in front of another huge window.

CARL (cont'd)
Where are we going?

VAN HELSING/ANNA
Through that window!

Carl turns around to see the window they're talking about, he pulls the pin on his contraption. Van Helsing and Anna each grab one of Carl's arms, on the run, and yank him out through the great glass window.

INT. CATACOMBS – NIGHT
Van Helsing, Anna, and Carl crash through the shower of glass and drop two stories down into a watery CATACOMB.

INT. STAIRCASE/HALLWAY – NIGHT
The huge door disintegrates as the vampires crash through it. They bound down the hallway. The contraption is sitting on the floor, it pops open, rays of ULTRA VIOLET LIGHT stream out. The vampires all melt screaming.

INT. CATACOMBS – NIGHT
Van Helsing, Anna, and Carl burst to the surface inside a large moldy catacomb filled with skulls and skeletons, the huge EXPLOSION OF LIGHT finishing above them as pieces of melted vampire splash down around them.

VAN HELSING
Carl, you're a genius.

CARL (a bit freaked out)
A genius with access to unstable chemicals.

Behind them, Igor YELLS commands in Hungarian as he and a dozen of the porcine Dwergi ride a LONGBOAT down a ramp. Frankenstein chained to the mast. Van Helsing immediately heads for the longboat.

Igor and the Dwergi drop their oars into the water and start to row. Van Helsing runs faster. Igor and the Dwergi paddle out of a tunnel and into the river. A huge grated GATE starts to drop down behind them. Igor pats Frankenstein on the head.

IGOR
Say goodbye to your friends.

Frankenstein BELLOWS angrily. Igor cackles.

IGOR (cont'd)
Because where we are taking you, only God and the devil know.

The metal gate SLAMS SHUT right in front of Van Helsing, cutting him off from the river, he splashes up to it and stares out through the grates. Frankenstein looks back at Van Helsing. Frankenstein's haggard face a mask of helplessness and hopelessness, looking forlorn and abandoned. Van Helsing stares at him and grits his teeth in determination.

VAN HELSING
I'll find you! . . . I'll get you back and set you free. I swear to god.

A huge DARK SHADOW swoops past, its talons scrape across the metal grating, SPARKS FLY.

DRACULA (O.S.)
God hasn't helped you in years, Van Helsing, why should he start now!?

We hear Aleera LAUGH as the two dark shadows fly away. Anna and Carl run up beside Van Helsing. Anna grabs him.

ANNA
Come on, we've got to beat them back to Castle Frankenstein.

Van Helsing whirls around and starts to go.

VAN HELSING
Yes, I've got to save that creature.

CARL (O.S.)
Van Helsing!

Van Helsing turns back to Carl, who is still staring out through the grate.

CARL (cont'd)
I cabled Rome earlier, to apprise them of our situation.

Van Helsing gives Carl a suspicious look.

VAN HELSING
And what did they say?

Carl turns to face him.

CARL
Even if you do somehow kill Dracula . . . Rome orders you to destroy Frankenstein as well.

Van Helsing's eyes darken, he starts to rev up.

VAN HELSING
He isn't evil.

CARL
Yes, but they said he isn't human either.

Van Helsing furiously closes in on Carl.

VAN HELSING
Do they know him? Have they talked with him? Who are they to judge!?

CARL
They want you to destroy him so he can never be used to harm humanity.

Van Helsing angrily grabs Carl by the throat and lifts him up off his feet.

VAN HELSING
And what of me? Did you tell them what I am to become? Did they tell you how to kill me? The correct angle of the stake as it enters my heart?! The exact measure of silver in each bullet!!

Van Helsing's voice has gotten incredibly deeper during this speech, his eyes have gone dark red and he's strangling Carl. Anna is already trying to rip the two men apart, but Van Helsing's strength is too much for her. Carl gasps:

CARL
No. . . . I . . . I left you out.

Van Helsing snaps out of it and lets him go. Carl drops to the ground, sucking air. Van Helsing stares down at him, feeling terribly, then he looks at his shaking hands, a whirlwind of emotions passing over his face, he clenches his hands into fists, then exhales deeply and looks at Anna.

VAN HELSING
It's starting.

INT. CASTLE FRANKENSTEIN LABORATORY – DAY
Van Helsing, Anna, and Carl run into the laboratory. It's empty, all of the lab equipment has been hurriedly removed.

VAN HELSING
They must have taken all the equipment to Dracula's lair.

ANNA
Then we've lost.

CARL
Dracula cannot bring his children to life until the sun sets. We still have time.

ANNA (incredulous)
"Time?" The sun sets in two hours, and we've been searching for him for more than four hundred years.

CARL
I wasn't around for those four hundred years, now was I?

EXT. MANOR VALERIOUS – DAY
The rays of the mid-day sun are trying to pry their way through the cloud-streaked sky over Manor Valerious. We can hear Van Helsing, Anna, and Carl pounding up a staircase.

VAN HELSING (O.S.)
So what did you learn?

INT. TOWER BEDROOM – DAY
Our heroes enter the tower bedroom where they come upon the mass of relics, artifacts, and texts.

CARL
That Count Dracula was actually the son of Valerious the Elder.

Carl looks at Anna.

CARL ((cont'd)
The son of you're ancestor.

Anna just shrugs, no big deal.

ANNA
Everybody knows that, what else?

CARL
Oh, uh, right. Well, it all started in 1462, when Dracula was murdered.

VAN HELSING
Does it say who murdered him?

CARL
No, just some vague reference to the Left Hand of God.

Van Helsing looks intrigued. Carl opens the elaborately inscribed SACRED LATIN TEXT.

CARL (cont'd)
Anyway, according to this when Dracula died he made a covenant with the devil.

Van Helsing and Anna jump in, guessing.

VAN HELSING
And was given a new life.

ANNA
But the only way to sustain that life was by drinking the blood of others.

CARL (annoyed)
Are you two going to let me tell the story?

VAN HELSING/ANNA
Sorry. Sorry.

CARL
Your ancestor, having sired this evil creature, went to Rome to seek forgiveness from God, that's when the bargain was made, Valerious the Elder was to kill Dracula in return for the eternal salvation of his entire family, right down the line all the way to you.

He points to Anna. Anna nods in understanding.

ANNA
But he couldn't do it. As evil as Dracula was, my ancestor could not kill his own son.

Carl points at some of the fantastical engravings on the relics and artifacts, helping tell the story:

CARL
So he banished Dracula to an icy fortress, sending him through a door from which there was no return.

ANNA
And then the devil gave him wings.

CARL
Yes.

VAN HELSING
All right, so where is this door?

CARL
I don't know, but when the old knight couldn't kill his son, he left clues, so that future generations might do it for him.

ANNA
That must be what my father was looking for in here, clues to the door's location.

An idea suddenly springs into Van Helsing's head.

VAN HELSING
The door . . . The door . . . of course!

He turns and races out of the room. Anna and Carl exchange a look, then haul-ass after Van Helsing.

INT. ARMORY – DAY
Van Helsing runs up to the massive floor-to-ceiling OIL PAINTING of Transylvania. Anna and Carl right behind him.

VAN HELSING
You said your father spent hours staring at this painting, trying to find Dracula's lair, I think you were right, quite literally.

Van Helsing checks where the frame meets the wall, but the frame is actually molded into the wall.

VAN HELSING (cont'd)
I think this is the door. He just didn't know how to open it.

Carl points to a LATIN INSCRIPTION on the painting.

CARL
Look! A Latin inscription. Maybe it works like that painting in the tower.

Carl starts mumbling the inscription in Latin. Anna steps up to Van Helsing

ANNA
If this was a door, my father would have opened it long ago.

Carl shoves a chair aside, revealing a missing piece of the painting.

CARL
I can't finish the inscription. There's a piece missing.

VAN HELSING
Your father didn't have this.

Van Helsing pulls out the torn piece of painted cloth.

ANNA
Where did you get that?

Van Helsing hands the painted piece of cloth to Carl.

VAN HELSING
Finish it.

Carl places it inside the missing piece of the map. *The torn piece is a perfect match.* Carl finishes the inscription.

CARL
Deum lacessat ac ianuam imbeat aperiri.

VAN HELSING
In the name of God, open this door.

And that's when the painting begins to change, starting at the frame line and spreading inward, a THICK CRYSTAL FROST washes over the painting, eating it up until the painting has completely dissolved, leaving an ANCIENT MIRROR in its place.

CARL
A mirror?

Anna stares at it, thinking hard.

ANNA
Dracula has no reflection in a mirror.

VAN HELSING
Why?

CARL
Maybe . . . maybe to Dracula, it's not a mirror at all.

Van Helsing reaches out to touch the mirror, his hand goes straight through it, vanishing inside it, he inhales sharply. Carl jumps.

CARL/ANNA
What? What?!

VAN HELSING
It's cold.

He pulls his hand out to reveal SNOWFLAKES in his palm.

VAN HELSING (cont'd)
And it's snowing.

Van Helsing grabs a TORCH out of a sconce on the wall, and prepares to step through.

VAN HELSING (cont'd)
See you on the other side.

CARL
Don't worry, we're behind you . . . not right behind you, but behind you.

Anna grabs his arm.

ANNA
Be careful.

Van Helsing gives her a nod, then steps straight through the mirror, vanishing inside it.

EXT. CASTLE DRACULA – DUSK
Van Helsing steps out of another ancient mirror, encased in a huge black OBELISK. It's snowing. A beat later, Anna steps through. They both look up. Chiselled out of a massive rock mountain is an enormous cathedral-like fortress; spires, turrets, gargoyles, the works. Covered in permafrost. Icicles everywhere. Carelessly

flung hither and yon are human skeletons. Something very evil lives here. THUNDER RUMBLES.

ANNA
Castle Dracula.

They look back at the mirror. Carl is nowhere in sight. They head for the castle. Behind them, Carl slowly seeps out of the mirror, eyes closed, he opens them to see the forbidding fortress. The sheer enormity of it terrifies him. He spins around and runs back into the mirror—wham! Face first, bounces off and lands on his ass. The mirror is a one-way ticket. Carl leaps up and scurries after them.

CARL
Wait up!

EXT. CASTLE DRACULA – NIGHT
They arrive at a massive door at the front of the ancient fortress, made of iron, rusted shut, covered in slippery ice. There's a TRANSOM at the top of it, but it's thirty feet up.

CARL
Do we have a plan? It doesn't have to be Wellington's at Waterloo, but some sort of plan would be nice.

VAN HELSING
We're going to go in there and stop Dracula.

ANNA
And kill anything that gets in our way.

Carl starts to back away.

CARL
Let me know how that goes.

Van Helsing grabs Carl and Anna by their collars and runs straight up, thirty feet, they go right through the transom.

INT. CASTLE DRACULA ENTRANCE HALL – NIGHT
The three of them land softly on the floor on the other side. Anna and Carl are shocked, they turn and look at Van Helsing.

CARL
Well, as grateful as I am to be out of the cold, that doesn't seem like a good thing.

Anna looks at Van Helsing, bent over in pain, his face and eyes are distorted into a vague resemblance of a wolf, and then it passes. They share a look.

Then he moves forward, a man on a mission. The whole place is a massive frozen foyer, and all of the incredibly high walls, pillars, and ceilings are covered in gooey COCOONS. Thousands of them. With electric wires sticking out of all of them.

ANNA
Oh my god, if he brings all of these to life . . .

CARL
. . . the world would be a smorgasbord.

And that's when Igor comes scurrying around a corner, a bundle of wires and electrodes in his hands, he skids to a stop, looking stunned as he sees Van Helsing.

IGOR
How? How did you? . . . It's impossible.

He quickly recovers his senses, drops everything and runs like hell. Van Helsing pumps one of the saw blades into his palm and throws it, it whistles through the air, catches Igor by his sleeve, and pins him to a rock wall.

IGOR (cont'd)
Please! Please don't kill me!

Van Helsing strides forward.

VAN HELSING
Why?

IGOR
Well, um, I . . .

He can't think of a good reason. Van Helsing rips the blade out of the wall, about to kill him. And then they hear Frankenstein BELLOW. Somewhere nearby. They look around. Right next to Igor is a window with metal bars. Van Helsing sees something moving inside it. It's a PULLEY with chains. He sticks his torch through the bars and looks down a SHAFT.

INT. CASTLE DRACULA – DUNGEON – NIGHT

Frankenstein is in a DUNGEON CELL encased in a huge BLOCK OF ICE, only his head and neck stick out, chains run through the block and attach up to the pulley. The shaft rises another thirty floors. From the top of the shaft a VOICE rings out:

> **DRACULA** (O.S.)
> Bring me the monster . . . !!

Dracula's voice ECHOES through the immense fortress as Igor snickers evilly.

INT. CASTLE DRACULA – ENTRANCE HALLWAY – DUSK

> **IGOR**
> My Master has awakened.

The pulley starts to rise. The chains snap taut. Frankenstein and the block of ice quickly lift up off the cell floor.

INT. CASTLE DRACULA – ENTRANCE HALLWAY – NIGHT

Van Helsing drops the torch and goes nuts, furiously yanking and pulling on the thick bars with incredible strength, they actually start to twist, but they're never going to give, even with the semi-insane look which has crept into his eyes. Anna tries to help, to no avail.

The block of ice continues its rise. Van Helsing collapses against the bars, the insane look seeps away, he's back to himself once again. Frankenstein comes eye-to-eye with him. The two beings look at each other, a real connection between the two of them. The look on Frankenstein's face softens.

> **FRANKENSTEIN**
> There is a cure.

Van Helsing is shocked.

> **VAN HELSING**
> What?

> **FRANKENSTEIN**
> Dracula, he has the cure, to remove the curse of the Werewolf.

Frankenstein continues up the shaft. Van Helsing desperately tries to stick his head through the bars, gaining one last look up at Frankenstein as he's hauled up.

> **FRANKENSTEIN** (cont'd)
> Go! Find the cure! Save yourself!

Anna grabs Van Helsing and pulls him back.

> **ANNA**
> Come on! You heard him! Let's find it.

Van Helsing looks at her, thinking hard.

> **VAN HELSING**
> Why does Dracula have a cure?

> **ANNA**
> I don't care.

> **VAN HELSING**
> I do. Why would he need one?

Van Helsing looks at Igor. Igor clamps his mouth shut. The CAMERA does a dramatic PUSH IN on Carl as his face fills with a dawning realization:

> **CARL**
> Because the only thing that can kill him . . . is a werewolf.

Van Helsing and Anna look at Carl. Carl smiles.

> **CARL** (cont'd)
> The painting. That's what it meant.

> **ANNA**
> But Dracula has used werewolves to do his biding for centuries.

> **CARL**
> Yes, but if one ever had the will to turn on him, he'd need a cure to remove the curse and make it human before it bit him.

The realization of this crashes down on them. Van Helsing turns to Igor and gestures to Anna and Carl.

> **VAN HELSING**
> You're going to take these two and lead them to it.

> **IGOR**
> No I'm not.

Van Helsing sticks the blade under Igor's chin. Igor smiles.

> **IGOR** (cont'd)
> Yes I am.

Carl steps up.

> **CARL**
> When the bell begins to toll midnight, you'll be able to kill Dracula, we just have to find the cure and get it into you before the final stroke.

Van Helsing pulls a small but extremely nasty-looking WEAPON out of his cloak. It looks like nail clippers designed by the Spanish Inquisition. He holds it up in front of Igor's face.

> **VAN HELSING**
> If they even suspect you're misleading them . . .

He hands the weapon to Anna.

> **VAN HELSING** (cont'd)
> . . . clip off one of his fingers.

> **ANNA**
> My pleasure.

Igor looks terrified, he gestures to the set of staircases.

> **IGOR**
> The stairs on the right, they lead to the black tower, that's where it is.

> **VAN HELSING**
> And the stairs on the left?

Igor hesitates. Van Helsing reaches for the "clippers."

> **IGOR**
> The Devil's tower! Devil's tower! That's where we reassembled the laboratory. Would I lie to you?

VAN HELSING
Not if you wanted to live.

Van Helsing turns to Carl.

VAN HELSING (cont'd)
If I'm not "cured" by the twelfth stroke of midnight . . .

He pulls a metal tube out of his cloak, snaps out into a SILVER STAKE, and hands it to Carl. Carl's eyes widen.

CARL
I don't think I could.

VAN HELSING
You must.

Carl nods, takes the stake, shares a look with Van Helsing, and then grabs Igor by the scruff of his neck and pulls him off towards the staircases.

CARL
Come on.

Van Helsing and Anna look into each other's eyes, both of them scared, both of them gearing up. Van Helsing has never been so concerned for another human being in his life.

VAN HELSING
Don't get killed.

Anna has never been so filled with conviction in her life.

ANNA
You still don't understand. It doesn't matter what happens to me. We must save my family.

She starts to go. Van Helsing pulls her back.

VAN HELSING
If you're late . . . run like hell.

She nods and starts to go. Van Helsing pulls her back again.

VAN HELSING (cont'd)
Don't be late.

She smiles and starts to go. Van Helsing pulls her back again, and then kisses her hard. She gives it right back to him, a real bodice ripper, she pulls herself away, stares deep into his smoldering eyes, then runs off after Carl.

INT. LABORATORY TOWER – NIGHT
The Dwergi are putting the final touches on the reassembly of Victor Frankenstein's equipment. Frankenstein himself is now welded into the iron pod, bellowing angrily. Dracula strides past, slamming all of the huge electrical switches on.

DRACULA
What are you complaining about?

The entire laboratory sparks to life. Spectacular arcs of electricity shoot up and down the walls between the dynamos. The gears kick in. The fan belts snap taut and start to spin.

DRACULA (cont'd)
This is why you were made, to prove that god is not the only one who can create life!

Dracula turns the flywheel. Frankenstein begins to rise.

DRACULA (cont'd)
And now you will give that life to my young.

INT. CASTLE DRACULA – RIGHT TOWER STAIRS – NIGHT
Van Helsing comes up the spiraling stone staircase and sees a large gash in the rock wall.

INT. CASTLE DRACULA – SHAFT – NIGHT

Van Helsing steps inside and sees CHAINS jangling in the middle of the dark shaft, he looks down at the fifteen-story drop. And then he jumps. He grabs the chains, swings wildly, dangling precariously, some of his weapons drop out of his cloak and fall. And then, with superhuman strength, agility and speed, Van Helsing starts to climb the chains.

INT. CASTLE DRACULA – ANTIDOTE TOWER – NIGHT

Igor leads Anna and Carl up the stairs to a landing with an arched doorway, the entrance to the Antidote Tower.

> **IGOR**
> There it is.

Inside the large room is a pedestal. On the pedestal is a GLASS JAR filled with a clear jelly-like goo, suspended in the goo is a SYRINGE. Igor starts to enter. Anna grabs him and holds him back.

> **ANNA**
> I'll go first.

Igor gives her a nasty look. Anna gives it back to him, then enters the tower, eyes on the alert, heading for the syringe. All the windows are barred shut. There is no other entrance.

Carl watches her, his eyes momentarily off Igor. Igor uses the moment, takes a quick step back, and with the heel of his boot, kicks Carl in the ass. Anna spins around in time to see Carl sprawl into the room. Igor cackles gleefully.

> **IGOR**
> Stay as long as you like.

He pulls a lever on the wall, a grated metal gate crashes down, locking Anna and Carl inside the tower. Igor scurries away laughing.

> **IGOR** (cont'd)
> Bye-bye!

INT. LABORATORY – NIGHT

All of the equipment is accelerating wildly.

The Dwergi are desperately trying to keep everything from spinning out of control. Dracula is in rapture as sparks rain down upon him.

Van Helsing climbs up out of the shaft and hides behind the shattered block of ice, which is being pelted and melted by raining sparks. Dynamos crackle. Pulleys whirl. Electrical arcs flash. Van Helsing looks up. Sixty feet above him is an OPEN SKYLIGHT, twenty feet above that is the POD apparatus.

EXT. CASTLE DRACULA – SKYLIGHT – NIGHT

Frankenstein struggles in the pod as LIGHTNING FLASHES across the sky above him.

INT. ANTIDOTE TOWER – NIGHT

Anna and Carl are staring at the syringe inside the jar of vile goo.

> **ANNA**
> Go ahead, grab it.

> **CARL**
> You go ahead and grab it. If there's one thing I've learned, it's never be the first one to stick your hand into a viscous material.

A hideous FACE lowers down right behind them. It's Aleera.

> **ALEERA**
> Smart boy.

Carl practically jumps out of his skin. Anna grabs Carl and jerks him back behind the huge jar. Aleera drops down with a smile.

> **ALEERA** (cont'd)
> Did I scare you?

> **CARL** (terrified)
> No.

> **ALEERA**
> Then maybe I need to try a little harder.

INT. LABORATORY – NIGHT

Van Helsing starts to climb STRAIGHT UP THE SHEER WALL. Grasping for

purchase in the grouting. Only someone with superhuman strength in their fingertips could do this.

A Dwerger on scaffolding turns around and comes face-to-face with Van Helsing, clinging to the wall like a fly. The Dwerger's goggles are up and we get our first glimpse of the hideous Dwergi eyes. Before the Dwerger can even scream, Van Helsing grabs him with one hand, slams him off the rock wall, then chucks him into the dark recesses of the laboratory.

INT. ANTIDOTE TOWER – NIGHT

Anna suddenly lashes out with her sword and knocks over the jar. It crashes to the floor, splattering some goo on Aleera. The vile goo burns like acid into her and right through the stone floor. Aleera HOWLS in pain and rage. Carl freaks.

> **CARL**
> See! What did I tell you!?

Anna gestures to the syringe rolling across the floor.

> **ANNA**
> Grab it! Grab it! Grab it!

Using the hem of his frock, Carl scoops up the syringe, it burns and smokes and he jumps and yelps, but he still manages to hold onto it. In the meantime, Anna has grabbed a piece of the glass and scooped up some of the goo. She runs and flings it at the bars of the gate. A hole melts through the bars.

> **ANNA** (cont'd)
> C'mon!

Carl races to the hole, the syringe smoking-up his frock. Anna shoves Carl out first.

> **ANNA** (cont'd)
> Go! Go! Go!

Carl races off down the hall. Before Anna can get out, a hand grabs her and spins her around. It's Aleera. The burns on her face HEAL.

> **ALEERA**
> You can't go until I say you can go.

ANNA
KEEP RUNNING CARL!

ALEERA
And I'll say you can go when you're dead.

Aleera grabs Anna and throws her across the floor. Anna skids across the room, her sabre goes flying.

EXT. CASTLE DRACULA – SKYLIGHT – NIGHT
Up on the pod Van Helsing comes eye-to-eye with Frankenstein. The WIND whips at them. LIGHTNING FLASHES. THUNDER ROARS. Van Helsing grabs one of the three metal straps welded onto the bolts riveted down Frankenstein's chest.

VAN HELSING
This is going to hurt.

FRANKENSTEIN (grits his teeth)
I am accustomed to pain.

Van Helsing nods, bad-to-the-bone.

VAN HELSING
Lets you know you're alive.

With his new strength, Van Helsing rips the first metal strap off. Frankenstein grimaces in pain. And that's when a BOLT OF LIGHTNING STRIKES the conductor above the pod. Van Helsing is catapulted into the air. Frankenstein roars in pain.

INT. LABORATORY – NIGHT
Dracula looks up as a BLAST OF ENERGY emanates from the pod down into the room and through the equipment, which instantly OVERLOADS, spitting FLAMES and SPARKS. One of the Dwergi is blown across the room, ON FIRE. Dracula smiles maniacally.

DRACULA
Give me LIFE!!!

The blast of energy surges out through every door, crack, and pore of the room.

INT. ENTRANCE HALL – NIGHT
The energy blast envelops the entrance hall washing over all the cocoons, which begin to UNDULATE with life.

EXT. SKYLIGHT – NIGHT
Van Helsing dangles from the edge of the tower, it's a sixty floor drop to an icy canyon below, electrical wires crackle and spit all around him. He starts to claw his way back up.

INT. ANTIDOTE TOWER – NIGHT
Anna staggers to her feet as Aleera strides towards her. Anna grabs a torch off the wall and lunges at Aleera's face. Aleera just blows it out. Anna quickly backs away. Aleera smiles, then one by one she blows out all of the torches in the room until the place goes PITCH BLACK.

EXT. TOWER BRIDGE – NIGHT
The weather has gone insane. Thunder, lightning, rain and wind whip down around Carl as he runs out onto an enormous ancient STONE BRIDGE

that connects the two towers. It's covered in huge potholes and barbed rubble. A LIGHTNING STRIKE hits one of the stone pilasters on the bridge. It's going to be a very difficult *six hundred yard dash*.

And that's when Igor runs out with his cattle prod. Carl jags out of the way as the prod slams into the railing right next to him, just missing him, spitting sparks.

EXT. SKYLIGHT – NIGHT
Van Helsing rips the second metal strap off of Frankenstein. Frankenstein grimaces in pain, then he sees something coming.

> **FRANKENSTEIN**
> Look out!

Van Helsing throws himself to the floor of the apparatus as once again LIGHTNING STRIKES the conductor above the pod. Frankenstein roars in pain.

INT. LABORATORY – NIGHT
Another energy blast surges through the room. Dracula lifts his arms and eyes to the sky in triumph.

> **DRACULA**
> One more bolt and my young shall live!

And then he sees Van Helsing high above him. Dracula scowls and TRANSFORMS into a HIDEOUS WINGED BEAST FROM HELL.

INT. ANTIDOTE TOWER – NIGHT
Pitch black. And then a lightning strike illuminates Anna, groping her way around the room, WE RACK FOCUS to see Aleera hanging upside down from the ceiling twenty feet behind her.

WE PUSH IN ON Aleera's gleaming face. And then go to her POV: Aleera can see perfectly in the dark. She watches as Anna gropes her way across the dark wall, heading for the gate.

EXT. TOWER BRIDGE – NIGHT
SPARKS explode off the tip of the cattle prod as it slams into a pilaster right next to Carl's head. Carl takes off running across the ancient bridge towards the distant tower. Igor chases after him with the sparking prod.

EXT. SKYLIGHT – NIGHT
Van Helsing rips the last metal strap off of Frankenstein. And that's when the hideous Winged Dracula Beast swoops up and rips into Van Helsing, throwing him back. Van Helsing bounces off the apparatus and drops—

INT. LABORATORY – NIGHT
—sixty feet down through the room, crashing through the equipment on his way. SPARKS FLY. FLAMES BLOW. Dwergi run.

EXT. SKYLIGHT – NIGHT
Frankenstein stands up, dazed, about to step out of the pod. Another BOLT OF LIGHTNING strikes the conductor. It lights Frankenstein up like a Christmas tree and catapults him through the air. An energy blast surges down into the lab.

INT. ENTRANCE HALL – NIGHT
And washes over the cocoons. The cocoons begin to EXPLODE. Hundreds and hundreds of the hideous pygmy bats burst out and swarm around the great hall.

INT. ANTIDOTE TOWER – NIGHT
Anna makes it to the gate. Lightning flashes, revealing Aleera standing on the other side of it, she punches Anna across the room. Anna slams into a wall and drops like a sack of potatoes, out cold.

EXT. SKYLIGHT – NIGHT
Frankenstein clings to the edge of the tower, struggling to hold on as electrical wires spark and spit all around him. He loses his grip and starts to drop. It's sixty stories down. He manages to grab a wire, which snaps loose and swings him down and across the castle, his legs kicking wildly.

EXT. TOWER BRIDGE – NIGHT
Carl runs like mad, weaving and bobbing as Igor tries to nail him with the cattle prod. Carl suddenly sees Frankenstein swinging on a wire, coming right at him. Carl dives to the ground as the wire whips over his head. The wire catches Igor across the chest and launches him out over the

railing. The wire then catches on a pilaster whipping Frankenstein into the bridge. Igor drops past him, screaming in terror on his long journey down to the icy valley below.

INT. ANTIDOTE TOWER – NIGHT
Anna groggily rolls over on the floor. Aleera steps up over her, then grabs her and lifts her up while TRANSFORMING into a huge winged bat.

INT. LABORATORY – NIGHT
Battered and bloody, Van Helsing staggers through the burning equipment, looking delirious.

EXT. TOWER BRIDGE – NIGHT
Carl looks over the railing. Sees Frankenstein hanging by the wire, dangling sixty stories up, losing his grip, sliding down the last five feet of the wire, now four feet, now three feet, two feet, one. He looks up at Carl.

> **FRANKENSTEIN**
> Help . . . me.

Carl is emotionally torn.

> **CARL**
> You're supposed to die.

Frankenstein grimaces, desperately clinging to life.

> **FRANKENSTEIN**
> I want to live.

Carl makes his decision.

> **CARL**
> All right! All right! Hold on! Hold on!

Carl sticks the syringe between his teeth, grabs the connector wire and pulls with all his might.

INT. ANTIDOTE TOWER – NIGHT
Anna can barely move, choking from the incredible grip Aleera has on her throat. Aleera's hideous face smiles.

> **ALEERA**
> Be happy in the knowledge that I shall weep over your dead body.

EXT. TOWER BRIDGE – NIGHT
Carl gives one last tug. The wire breaks loose from the pilaster. Frankenstein swings away from the bridge and arcs up towards a barred window on the side of the Antidote Tower.

INT. ANTIDOTE TOWER – NIGHT
Aleera's fangs distend, she leans into bite Anna's neck. And that's when Frankenstein crashes through the barred window and slams into them. Anna is knocked free.

INT. LABORATORY – NIGHT
The huge Winged Beast strides through the flames, then TRANSFORMS back into Dracula, a smile on his lips.

> **DRACULA**
> You're too late, my friend! My children live!

Van Helsing backs away, really messed up.

> **VAN HELSING**
> Then the only way to kill them . . .

He looks out through a window at the old CLOCK TOWER.

> **VAN HELSING** (cont'd)
> . . . is to kill you.

A look of pure confidence fills Dracula's face.

> **DRACULA**
> That is correct.

A deranged look fills Van Helsing's face.

> **VAN HELSING**
> So be it.

EXT. ANTIDOTE TOWER – NIGHT
Anna looks back into the tower. Aleera lunges at her, but Frankenstein grabs her. Anna starts to head back to help Frankenstein.

> **FRANKENSTEIN**
> No! Go help Van Helsing.

Frankenstein throws Aleera across the room, then looks at Anna.

> **FRANKENSTEIN** (cont'd)
> Now!

Anna looks him in the eyes.

> **ANNA**
> Thank you.

Frankenstein nods and turns back to Aleera, who flies across the room and tackles him. Anna scrambles back out the window.

EXT. TOWER BRIDGE – NIGHT

A bolt of lightning suddenly rips a huge GAPING HOLE out of the bridge near Carl, blocking him from continuing forward. It's a twenty-foot leap or a sixty-story drop. He looks back and sees Anna crawling out of the smashed window.

> **CARL**
> Anna! I need some help!

Anna clings to the wind-whipped wall, trying not to get blown into the precipice.

> **ANNA**
> Now is not a good time, Carl!!

INT. LABORATORY – NIGHT

As Dracula moves in on Van Helsing, Van Helsing looks out a window to the CLOCK-TOWER. The BIG HAND slams forward. It is now exactly one minute to midnight. The clock CHIMES. Van Helsing's whole body suddenly CONVULSES. Insanity pours into his eyes. Dracula looks perplexed. Van Helsing GROANS:

> **VAN HELSING**
> One.

Van Helsing TRANSFORMS into the biggest, sexiest, most bad-assed Werewolf ever. Dracula looks stunned.

> **DRACULA**
> No. . . . This . . . this is not right.
> *(furious)*
> This can not be!

EXT. TOWER BRIDGE – NIGHT

Carl looks from the clock tower to Anna.

> **CARL**
> Hurry!

Anna leaps out and grabs the same electrical wire that Frankenstein used. The wire HISSES and SPARKS as Anna is swung down across the castle. The CLOCK CHIMES.

> **ANNA**
> Two!

INT. LABORATORY – NIGHT

Dracula cautiously backs off as the huge Werewolf collects itself and moves towards him. For the first time in his long life, Dracula actually looks nervous, he plays for time.

> **DRACULA**
> You and I are part of the same grand game, Gabriel. But we need not find ourselves on opposite sides of the board.

EXT. TOWER BRIDGE – NIGHT

The clock CHIMES. Carl steps up to the edge of the bridge, he's going to throw Anna the syringe.

> **CARL**
> Three!

Anna switches wires in mid-air as she rockets across the castle. Carl aims and throws the syringe. Anna grabs it! Then arcs up towards the Laboratory Tower.

INT. LABORATORY – NIGHT

The Werewolf LUNGES at Dracula. Dracula whirls around, becoming the Winged Beast, he flies up the wall, heading for the open skylight. The Werewolf bounds after him, ripping its way straight up the sheer rock, it leaps out and grabs the Winged Beast. Both creatures crash down into the equipment.

EXT. TOWER BRIDGE – NIGHT

The clock CHIMES as Anna arcs up towards the Laboratory Tower. And that's when Aleera swoops down and cuts the wire. Anna is thrown off. She crashes onto a ledge of the tower.

INT. LABORATORY – NIGHT

Dracula leaps up first and backs away.

> **DRACULA**
> You're being used Gabriel. As was I. But I escaped, and so can you!

The Werewolf springs at Dracula. Dracula becomes the Winged Beast and desperately uses his four razor sharp appendages to claw at the Werewolf. The Werewolf howls in pain, then lashes out and rips away at

the Beast. The Beast shrieks, then throws itself up into the rafters and becomes Dracula, his arm is torn and limp. The clock CHIMES.

DRACULA (cont'd)
I know who you are. Who controls you. Join me! Join me and I'll cut the strings that play you! I'll give you your life back!

EXT. TOWER BRIDGE – NIGHT
Anna clambers up onto a ledge just as Aleera lands next to her. Anna starts backing up the precarious perch as Aleera closes in. WE PAN UP to the FULL MOON and see CLOUDS ABOUT TO OBSCURE IT.

INT. LABORATORY – NIGHT
The Werewolf looks insanely hungry as it closes in on Dracula, who is desperately backing away.

DRACULA
Don't you understand!? Four hundred years ago we were friends. Partners! Brothers!

The clock CHIMES. The Werewolf leaps at him. Dracula becomes the Beast and desperately tries to fly away, but he's too damaged. The Werewolf grabs him by the throat, about to kill him, *and that's when the Werewolf turns back into Van Helsing.* Van Helsing quickly staggers back. Dracula looks out at the roiling clouds obscuring the moon, then he looks at Van Helsing. That old confident glint fills Dracula's eyes.

DRACULA (cont'd)
Did I mention that it was you who murdered me?

EXT. TOWER BRIDGE – NIGHT
The clock CHIMES. Anna backs up against a wall on the ledge, trapped. Aleera steps in for the kill.

ALEERA
Your blood shall make me even more beautiful. What do you think of that?

A SILVER STAKE suddenly impales her through the chest. Aleera shrieks. Anna looks over at the bridge, to where Carl has crawled down between the girders, then she looks back at Aleera, who is staring at her in horror and starting to rot.

ANNA
I think if you're going to kill somebody, kill them, don't stand around talking about it.

Aleera bursts into rot, the silver stake is flung into a beam right next to Carl's head. The clock CHIMES. Carl looks up at the clock.

CARL
How many is that!? How many is that!?

Anna is already racing up the parapet.

ANNA
Eight!

INT. LABORATORY – NIGHT
Van Helsing desperately backs off through the FLAMING, SPARKING equipment as Dracula slowly moves in on him.

DRACULA
All I wanted was life, Gabriel . . . now I'll have to take yours.

Dracula holds up his left hand, *his ring finger has long ago been CUT OFF.*

DRACULA (cont'd)
And I'll take my ring back as well.

The clock CHIMES. Van Helsing backs up into a wall, trapped, breathing hard, the two men stare at each other. Dracula's bicuspids distend into long fangs.

DRACULA (cont'd)
Don't be afraid, Gabriel, now I will give you back your life, your memory.

And then through a window, Van Helsing sees the clouds about to fully reveal the full moon. The clock CHIMES.

VAN HELSING
Some things are best left forgotten.

Van Helsing becomes the Werewolf. He lunges, grabs Dracula and CHOMPS into his throat. Dracula CRIES OUT in agony.

Dracula starts shriveling and decaying and wasting away until there is nothing left but charred remains burning into the floor. The clock CHIMES.

INT. ENTRANCE HALL – NIGHT
All of the pygmy bats shriek in horror and then explode into black goo.

INT. LABORATORY – NIGHT
Anna bursts into the room and races at the Werewolf's back, syringe in hand, ready to stab him. The clock CHIMES.

ANNA
Twelve.

The Werewolf spins around and sees Anna coming. He POUNCES. FANGS and CLAWS. Anna SCREAMS. The Werewolf tackles Anna. They crash down onto a couch. Carl runs in and skids to a stop, the Werewolf's back is to him, but he can see that it's alive and on top of Anna.

CARL
Midnight.

Carl is devastated. He lifts up the silver stake.

CARL (cont'd)
God forgive me.

He runs forward and swings the stake down at the Werewolf's back. At the last millisecond the Werewolf spins around and grabs Carl's wrist, stopping him short. Carl is terrified, he stares at the Werewolf. The Werewolf stares back, then turns slightly to reveal the SYRINGE sticking out of its chest, *empty.* The Werewolf lets go of Carl. Carl stumbles back. The Werewolf rips the empty syringe out of its chest, throws it away, then looks down at Anna. Her eyes are wide open.

CARL (cont'd)
She's dead.

And then WE CUT TO one of the most iconographic SHOTS in the whole movie: the FULL MOON shines in through an arched stone window, which frames the Werewolf, who is crouched over our gorgeous heroine, sprawled dead across a broken couch.

WE SLOWLY PUSH IN as the Werewolf tilts its head back and BAYS AT THE MOON, a long, mournful HOWL, it slowly TRANSFORMS back into Van Helsing, CRYING OUT at the moon in anguish. . . .

EXT. MOUNTAIN TOP – DAWN
Carl READS from the Bible, tears on his cheeks. Van Helsing, carrying a torch, steps up to a funeral pyre. He stares down at Anna, lying on the pyre, looking beautiful. WE CUT WIDE to see that they are on a bluff overlooking the SEA.

EXT. SEA – DAWN
A dark figure paddles a makeshift raft out to sea. It's Frankenstein. He looks back up to the bluff to see the flaming pyre IGNITE. Frankenstein doffs his hat in respect, sighs heavily, then turns back around and continues paddling.

EXT. MOUNTAIN TOP – NIGHT
The glow from the flames flickers off Van Helsing's sad face as he stares down at the ground. Carl still reading.

The SMOKE from the funeral pyre suddenly FORMS A PICTURE OF ANNA'S FACE. Tendrils of smoke waft out, like long smoky fingers they touch Van Helsing's chin and lift it up. Van Helsing sees her. Anna smiles. Then her face starts to float up into the dawn sky along with the rest of the smoke.

Van Helsing is shocked, he staggers forward, as if to follow.

Anna's face is suddenly surrounded by the vague faces of her mother, her father, her brother Velkan, and many other welcoming family members. Her father gives her a hug. Her mother starts to comb her hair.

Carl smiles as he steps up and puts his hand on Van Helsing's shoulder.

Anna gives Van Helsing one last look, her radiant eyes beaming with happiness, and then she and all of her family start to ascend into the glowing dawn sky.

Van Helsing stares upward, devastated.

And then in one final glorious moment, Anna and her family swoop up into the sky and blend with the fading stars.

WE PUSH IN on Van Helsing's face as the look in his eyes changes, from devastated loss, to a gentle look of peace. We can see that he is truly happy for Anna. . . .

DISSOLVE TO:

EXT. WHEAT FIELD – DAWN
Van Helsing and Carl riding two black stallions across an endless golden wheat field, heading off into a new dawn.

FADE OUT.

THE END

CREDITS

UNIVERSAL presents

VAN HELSING

Written and Directed by
STEPHEN SOMMERS

In Memory of My Dad

Produced by
STEPHEN SOMMERS   BOB DUCSAY

Executive Producer
SAM MERCER

Director of Photography
ALLEN DAVIAU, ASC

Production Designer
ALLAN CAMERON

Film Editors
BOB DUCSAY   KELLY MATSUMOTO

HUGH JACKMAN   KATE BECKINSALE

RICHARD ROXBURGH, DAVID WENHAM,
SHULER HENSLEY, ELENA ANAYA,
WILL KEMP, KEVIN J. O'CONNOR,
ALUN ARMSTRONG, SILVIA COLLOCA,
JOSIE MARAN, TOM FISHER, SAMUEL WEST

Casting by
PRISCILLA JOHN, CDG
ELLEN LEWIS
JOANNA COLBERT

Music Composed and Conducted by
ALAN SILVESTRI

Costume Designers
GABRIELLA PESCUCCI
CARLO POGGIOLI

Special Makeup Created by GREG CANNOM

Visual Effects Supervisors
BEN SNOW
SCOTT SQUIRES

Animation Supervisor DANIEL JEANNETTE

A STEPHEN SOMMERS Film

156

Unit Production Manager..............JOANN PERRITANO
First Assistant Director ....ARTIST ROBINSON
Second Assistant Director.............DEANNA STADLER

CAST
Van Helsing .... HUGH JACKMAN
Anna Valerious............................KATE BECKINSALE
Count Vladislaus Dracula ....RICHARD ROXBURGH
Carl....................................DAVID WENHAM
Frankenstein's Monster ....SHULER HENSLEY
Aleera...ELENA ANAYA
Velkan..WILL KEMP
Igor..............................KEVIN J. O'CONNOR
Cardinal Jinette ....ALUN ARMSTRONG
Verona ....SILVIA COLLOCA
Marishka ....JOSIE MARAN
Top Hat ....TOM FISHER
Dr. Victor Frankenstein ....SAMUEL WEST
Mr. Hyde ....ROBBIE COLTRANE
Doctor Jekyll ....STEPHEN H. FISHER
Barmaid..............................DANA MORAVKOVA
Opera Singer ....ZUZANA DURDINOVA
Gendarme...........................JAROSLAV VIZNER
Villager......................................MAREK VASUT
Vampire Child ....SAMANTHA SOMMERS
Dracula's Ball Performers ....DOREL MOIS
MARIANNA MOIS
LAURENCE RACINE
PATRICE WOJCIECHOWSKI

Stunt Coordinator .................................R.A. RONDELL
Asst. Stunt Coordinator /
   Fight Coordinator ....CHAD STAHELSKI

Stunt Doubles...........................RICHARD BRADSHAW
TROY BROWN, KARIN SILVESTRI COYE,
MIKE GUNTHER, MIKE JUSTUS, DAVID LEITCH,
MATT McCOLM, DANNY WYNANDS

Stunts ....SANDY BERUMEN-JUSTUS,
DEBBIE CARRINGTON, LAURA DASH,
CHRISTIAN J. FLETCHER, GRANT FLETCHER,
TAD GRIFFITH, JOSEPH GRIFFO,
FREDDIE HICE, MARTIN KLEBBA, HEATHER KRAFT,
OAKLEY LEHMAN, BILLY LUCAS, ROBERT MARRS,
HEIDI MONEYMAKER, BOB McDOUGALL,
MARIO MUNOZ, MARK MUNOZ, MICHAEL MUNOZ,
DOUGLAS NEITHERCUT, LARRY NICHOLAS,
BOBBY PORTER, MARK POVINELLI, TIMOTHY
RIGBY, DEBBY ROSS RONDELL, MISTY ROSAS,
DEEP ROY, DAVID SCHULTZ, DOUGLAS SNIVELY,
MONTY STUART, CARLY THOMAS, TIM TRELLA,
AARON WALTERS, TROY WOOD, DANA M. WOODS

Second Unit Director ....GREG MICHAEL
Visual Effects Producer......................JENNIFER BELL

ILM Character Design Group..........CARLOS HUANTE,
BRIAN KALIN O'CONNELL,
DEREK THOMPSON,
WAYNE LO, DANNY WAGNER
Design Supervisor......................DAVID NAKABAYASHI
ILM Visual Effects Producer............GRETCHEN LIBBY
ILM Visual Effects Associate
   Producer......................JEANMARIE KING

Additional Animation Supervisor ....HAL HICKEL
Visual Effects Art Director.........CHRISTIAN ALZMANN

Associate Visual Effects
   Producer............................JOSEPH GROSSBERG
Matte Painting Supervisor......................SYD DUTTON
Film Editor .... JIM MAY

Sound Mixers...........LESLIE SHATZ, DAVID PARKER,
DENNIS SANDS

Associate Producer ....ARTIST ROBINSON

Choreographer ....DEBRA BROWN
Dialect Coach ....JESS PLATT

Art Directors........................STEVE ARNOLD,
KEITH P. CUNNINGHAM, TONY READING,
GILES MASTERS
Assistant Art Directors ....ALEX CAMERON,
DAWN SWIDERSKI, DAWN SNYDER
Illustrator ....SIMON MURTON
Visual Consultant............STEPHEN FORREST SMITH
Art Department Coordinator.............WYLIE Y. GRIFFIN
Asset Coordinator.............................MICHAEL HEATH
Set Decorators...........CINDY CARR, ANNA PINNOCK
Assistant Set Decorator ....JON DANNIELLS
Set Decoration Coordinator ....LINDA GRIFFIS
On Set Dresser......................GREGORY P. ALCUS
Set Dresser / Gang Boss ....DAVID MILSTEIN
Leadman ....SHANE REED
Drapery Foreman ....RUBEN ABARCA
Set Designers.........LUKE FREEBORN, JANN ENGEL,
HARRY E. OTTO, EASTON SMITH,
ERIC SUNDAHL
Model Maker ....JASON MAHAKIAN
Property Masters ....DAVID BALFOUR
STEVEN B. MELTON

Camera Operator......................PAUL C. BABIN, S.O.C.
1st Assistant A Camera ....JIMMY JENSEN
2nd Assistant A Camera.....................NICK SHUSTER
B Camera Operator................TOM CONNOLE, S.O.C.
1st Assistant B Camera ....MARK SANTONI
2nd Assistant B Camera.....................ROGER WALL
Libra Head Technician ....GREG SCHMIDT
SteadiCam Operator................................CRAIG FIKSE
1st Assistant SteadiCam ....ALAN COHEN
Loader...TONY MULLER
Camera Production Assistant ....KEVIN BRITTON
Video Assist.........................MICHAEL J. HOGAN
Production Sound Mixer ....CHRIS MUNRO
Boom Operator................ANTHONY ORTIZ-QUINOES
Cableman...ROCKY QUIROZ

Production Coordinator ....JENNIFER CONROY
Assistant Coordinator ....MATTHEW HIRSCH
Production Secretary......................KELLY E. NORRIS
2nd 2nd Assistant
   Director ....MARIA BATTLE-CAMPBELL
Script Supervisor.........................SYLVIE CHESNEAU

Gaffer ....LARRY WALLACE
Best Boy ....ADAM CHAMBERS
Electricians .... JEFFREY AMARAL, JASON LEEDS,
JOHN LINARES, GEORGE MacDONALD,
WILLIAM MAYBERRY, GREG PATTERSON,
JASON SANTELLI, NOAH SHAIN,
LARRY WALLACE, JR., MICHAEL YOPE
Rigging Gaffer................................DANA M. ARNOLD
Best Boy Rigging.................................RICK SENTENO
Key Grip ....JAMES SHELTON
Best Boy Grip..KYLE CARDEN
Dolly Grips ....RICK CARDEN, GARY BEAIRD
Grips ....RICHARD ARTMAN, CRAIG BROWN,
SCOTT CARDEN, JOE KELLY, LONNIE LESLIE,
PABLO SANTIAGO, MIKE SIMKO, DAVE WALKER
Key Rigging Grip...............................RICK N. PRATT
Best Boy Rigging.................................HILARY KLYM
Special Effects Coordinator ....THOMAS L. FISHER
On-Set SFX Coordinator ....SCOTT R. FISHER

Special Effects Foremen ....RONALD D. GOLDSTEIN
MARIO VANILLO
SFX Office Coordinator ....KATRISSA PETERSON
Effects Technicians ....RYAN ARNDT,
STEVE AUSTIN, BILL COBB, MATT DOWNEY,
JOHN J. DOWNEY, MANNY EPSTEIN,
RONALD B. EPSTEIN, JOHN FLEMING,
RAYMOND HOFFMAN, JOSEPH JUDD,
BRUCE KHTEIAN, JAY B. KING,
BRUCE KUROYAMA, ROLAND LOEW, JOE LOVE,
BRUCE MINKUS, BRYAN PHILLIPS,
ALAN RIFKIN, JAMES ROLLINS,
GLENN THOMAS, LEO SOLIS, DOUG ZIEGLER,
ROBERT SLATER, OSCAR ORONA,
AGUSTIN TORAL, RANDY SCHWEISOW

Associate Costume
Designer.....................MASSIMO CANTINI PARRINI
Costume Supervisor ....NICK SCARANO
Key Costumers..............................GREGORY B. PENA
RICHARD SCHOEN
Set Costumers................................LAURA BAKER,
NANCY SMYTKA, CATHERINE PENA,
SILVIA RAIANO, JORGE J. GONZALEZ,
SERENA FIUMI, RENATA RYSAVA
Costume Coordinator ....RIZIA ORTOLANI
Workshop Head ....CONCETTA IANNELLI
Workshop Mistress......................SILVIA GUIDONI
Workshop Master ....SALVATORE SALZANO
Dying Labour................................SERAFINO PELLEGRINO
Aging Labour...............................KAREL VESELY
Workshop Assistants...........ROSSANA NICOLETTA,
LUCA CANFORA, JIRINA EISENHAMEROVA,
LUCIE HEFNEROVA, LUCIE KRAUSOVA,
JANA SUBRTOVA
Leather Workman.................................GIANNI FIUMI
Metal & Jewels Workman ....GIOVANNI INDOVINO
Head Women Costume Cutter.......ADRIANA MATTIOZZI
Head Men Costume Cutter ....GIAMPIETRO GRASSI
Tailor ....HOSSEIN NAMDAR
Ager / Dyer ....PHYLLIS THURBER-MOFFITT

Department Head Makeup ....NENA SMARZ
Co-Department Heads – Makeup ....ANGELA LEVIN
STEPHEN M. KELLEY
Co-Department Heads – Hair .SUSAN V. KALINOWSKI,
ELLE ELLIOTT, KARL WESSON
Ms. Beckinsale's Makeup Artist............VASILIOS TANIS
Lead Hair Stylist / Designer.....COLLEEN CALLAGHAN
Ms. Beckinsale's Hair Stylists ....SUSAN LIPSON
VONI HINKLE

Creature Concept Artists ....CRASH MCCREERY,
PATRICK TATOPOULOS, GERALD BROM

Environmental Concept Art ....HATCH
Special Makeup Effects
Created by ....KEITH VANDERLAAN'S
CAPTIVE AUDIENCE PRODUCTIONS, INC.

Effects Production Supervisor.....................BRIAN SIPE
Production Supervisor ....MARY KIM
Mold Dept. Supervisor ....ARTHUR PIMENTEL
Art Dept............MARTIN ASTLES, THOMAS M. BAXA,
KEVIN BRENNAN, RON BROWN,
JOHN M. DONAHUE, GLEN HANZ,
ANTHONY KOEHL, TIMOTHY LARSEN,
RAY SANTOLERI, CONSTANTINE SEKERIS,
MILES TEVES, MARIO TORRES JR.,
TODD TUCKER
Effects Technician........................HOWARD E. ADAMS,
DIAN D. BACHAR, KEN L. BANKS,
ANTHONY A. BARLOW, BRYAN BLAIR,

CHRIS W. CERA, PETER A. CHEVAKO,
BARRY D. CRANE, KEN CULVER,
MICHAEL P. DEL ROSSA, CONSUELO DURAN,
JACK A. FIRMAN, DAVID FISHER,
LISA L. FORNADLEY, NATHAN E. FRANSON,
CHRISTOPHER GALLAHER, SONNY GONZALEZ,
CHRIS S. HAMPTON, TIM JARVIS, JOHN KIM,
KRISTEN E. LOBSTEIN, BRIAN MECK,
VERENA MERCENIER, MARK NIEMAN,
LINDA D. NOTARO, MICHAEL O'BRIEN,
MIMI PALAZON, JAMES PARR,
GARY R. PAWLOWSKI, TED A. PENDERGRAFT,
MICHAEL PETERSON, ROBERT RAMOS,
SAEID RASTEGAR, COLIN D. RECCHIO,
WILLIAM E. RITTER, SAMUEL SAINZ,
TERRY SANDIN, LETICIA D. SANDOVAL,
JOHN F. SHEA, BRIAN VANDORN
Hair Technicians ....JUSTIN G. DITTER,
NATASCHA LADEK, DEBORAH A. GALVEZ,
CONSTANCE L. GRAYSON, ROBERT KRETSCHMER
Operations Managers ....HARVEY LOWRY
ALEXEI O'BRIEN
Production Coordinators ....KENNETH E. GRASSI
SHARON KELLY-RUSSO
Assistant to Mr. VanderLaan ....MICHAL GREGUS
Assistant to Mr. Sipe.................CHRISTINE N. REGAN
Assistant to Ms. Kim ....YVONNE JIMENEZ
Photographers ....CARMEN Y. AVILA,
CHRISTOPHER A. LOZANO, CHUCK ZLOTNICK
Production Assistant.........................SEAN P. NORTON
Production Consultant ....GARY GROSS
Effects Technician ....JERRY D. CONSTANTINE
Production Assistant...........GREGORY J. GOERTZEN
Additional Prosthetics ..............W.M. CREATIONS, INC.

Location Manager ....JAY TRAYNOR
Key Assistant Location Manager ...... RICK M. POYNER
Assistant Location Manager .....JOSEPH L. AKERMAN, JR.

Production Controller ....NICOLE FURIA

Location Accountant.................................ERIC LAYNE
First Assistant Accountant ....RICHARD CASTRO
Second Assistant
Accountants ....CAROLE HUMPHREYS,
MAHNAZ MAHDAVI,
JENNIFER TAMEZ, LAURA TIZ
Construction Accountant ....CHARLES ARAKI
2nd Unit Accountant ....JANETTE EVANS
Payroll...DAVID C. ROMANO
Casting Assistant ....FAITH ALLBESON
Extras Casting ....BACKGROUND PLAYERS

Extras Casting Coordinator ....JUDY COOK
Unit Publicist...GUY ADAN
Still Photographer....................................FRANK MASI
Assistant to Mr. Sommers ....JESSE PECKHAM
Assistants to Mr. Ducsay..........MATTHEW STUECKEN
RYAN LANDELS
Assistant to Mr. Mercer ....TEGAN JONES
Assistant to Mr. Jackman....................JOHN PALERMO
Assistant To Ms. Beckinsale ....MELISSA COGGIOLA
Assistant to Mr. Roxburgh ....MAIA HORNIAK
Sommers Company Assistant.............DINAH HUTSON
Fitness Trainers..................................MICHAEL RYAN
SCOTT McELROY
Production Office
Assistants ....RYAN G. MININGHAM,
MICHAEL M. PIEHLER, KEITH RAUCH
DGA Trainee ....JEFFREY HUNT
Key Set Production Assistant.....MICHAEL J. MUSTERIC
Set Production Assistants ....JASON HARITON
CHAD SAXTON

Transportation Coordinator..........RANDY MUSSELMAN
Transportation Captain ....GLENN MATHIAS
Transportation Co-Captain ....DOUG MILLER
Construction Coordinator.......................BUTCH WEST
General Foremen ....BROOK MANSBRIDGE
DAVID GABRIELLI
Propmaker Foremen ....THOMAS DIVALERIO,
CALVIN MANGUM, BOB McDONALD,
KURT MILLER, ROBERT SIMPSON,
TODD YOUNG
Propmaker Gangbosses ....LLOYD BUSHWELL,
SEAN GALLAGHER, RODNEY HIGGINS,
RON MONTGOMERY, CHARLES POKIPALA III,
THOMAS RITCHOTTE, DAVE ROZO
Welding Foreman ....FRANCIS WHITE
Lead Labor Foreman ....PHILLIP VARGAS
Labor Foremen.............................SERGIO ACEVEDO,
RAINER WOLF, DARREN WOOLEY
Labor Gangboss ....JOHNNY McINTYRE
Lead Plasterer ....ALEXANDER SCUTTI
Plasterer Foremen...........................LUKE ADKINS,
MICHAEL CARROLL, BRIAN FERNANDEZ,
ARTURO GUZMAN, ADAM SCUTTI,
JARED TREPPEPI, BARRY VINE
Plasterer Gangbosses ....SALVADOR ANAYA,
ANTHONY COPE, MATTHEW FUCHS,
CARLO PEREZ
Toolman ....ERIC GIESE
Paint Supervisor ....ROBERT DANTE DENNE
Paint Foreman ....THOMAS O'BRIEN
Standby Painter ....ROBERT E. DENNE
Lead Sculptor ....JAMIE MILLER
Sculptor Gangbosses ....YANN DENOUAL,
CHRIS HOPKINS, KEVIN MARKS, DAVID TYE
Craft Service ....BRUCE MORIN
Caterers ....FOR STARS CATERING

Visual Effects Coordinators ....CONNIE KENNEDY,
CELIA HALIQUIST
VFX On-Set Coordinator ....JAMES MADIGAN
VFX Post Prod. Coordinator .....CHRISTOPHER CRAM
Previsualization Supervisor.............RPIN SUWANNATH
Previsualization Artists ....SCOTT MEADOWS
MICHAEL MAKARA
JOHN F. LEE

Post Production Supervisor ....SEAN STRATTON

First Assistant Editor...................TZARINA V. EDILLON
First Assistant Film Editors ....MICHAEL D. GAY
JOSH CAMPBELL
Second Assistant Film Editor ....RAY BUSHEY
Assistant Editors - Prague...............MARTIN HUBACEK
MICHAEL SHERMAN
Apprentice Film Editor ....TAMARON DAWN GREENE
Editorial Production Assistants..................NICK CONTI
VACLAV SRAMEK
Post Production Accountant............LISA JEAN FELSKI

Supervising Sound Editors.....PER HALLBERG, MPSE,
KAREN BAKER LANDERS

ADR Supervisor ....CHRIS JARGO
Foley Supervisor ....CRAIG S. JAEGER, MPSE
Assistant Sound Editors .....TONY R. NEGRETE, MPSE
PHILIP D. MORRILL, BOB BOWMAN
Sound Effects Editors...........DINO R. DIMURO, MPSE,
CHRISTOPHER ASSELLS, MPSE,
EZRA DWECK, DANIEL HEGEMAN,
PETER STAUBLI, BRUCE TANIS, BRYAN BOWEN,
SCOTT SANDERS, HARRY COHEN
Dialog Editors...................................KIMAREE LONG,
FREDERICK H. STAHLY, MPSE

CREDITS

ADR Editors ....MICHELLE PAZER, ANNA MACKENZIE, ZACK DAVIS, VICKIE ROSE SAMPSON, THOMAS G. WHITING
Foley Editor.....................................LOU KLEINMAN
Foley by ....ONE STEP UP, INC.
Foley Artists.....................................DAN O'CONNELL JOHN CUCCI
Foley Mixer ....JAMES ASHWILL
ADR Mixers.....................................GREG STEELE, CHARLEEN RICHARDS-STEEVES, BOBBY JOHANSON, PETER GLEAVES
ADR Recordists............CHRISTOPHER FITZGERALD, DAVID LUCARELLI
BRIAN GALLAGHER ....ALEX BEDDOW
Additional Sound Mixer...................MICHAEL KELLER
Recordists.....................................DREW WEBSTER, CRAIG MANN, GARY SIMPSON

Special Visual Effects & Animation by
INDUSTRIAL LIGHT & MAGIC
a Lucasfilm Ltd. Company
Marin County, California

Computer Graphics Supervisors ......CRAIG HAMMACK, CURT MIYASHIRO, DOUG SMYTHE
Compositing Supervisors...........MARSHALL KRASSER GREG MALONEY
Creature Supervisor ....TIM MCLAUGHLIN
Animation Associate Supervisor.........STEVE NICHOLS
Animation Associate Producer ....JULIE D'ANTONI
Sequence Supervisors ....JEFFREY BENEDICT, IAN CHRISTIE, RAUL ESSIG, CARL FREDERICK, JEREMY GOLDMAN, ROBERT HOFFMEISTER, HAYDEN LANDIS, SEAN MACKENZIE, TIA MARSHALL, PATRICK MYERS, NIGEL SUMNER, JOHN WALKER, THOMAS ZILS
Sabre Supervisor ....GRADY COFER
Animation Sequence Supervisors ....TIMOTHY HARRINGTON MIGUEL FUERTES
Technical Animation Supervisor ....LESLIE FULTON
Digital Model Supervisors..............ANDREW CAWRSE, FRANK GRAVATT, BRUCE HOLCOMB
Viewpaint Supervisors ....JEAN-CLAUDE LANGER JEAN BOLTE
Lead CG Layout Artists.................TERRY CHOSTNER MARLA NEWALL
Digital Paint and Roto Supervisor..........KATIE MORRIS
Lead Digital Matte Artist...............BRETT NORTHCUTT
Visual FX Editors ....DAVID TANAKA NICOLAS ANASTASSIOU
Digital Color Timing Supervisor.....BRUCE VECCHITTO
TDs......................JOAKIM ARNESSON, JOEL ARON, KEVIN BARNHILL, KATHLEEN BEELER, MATTHEW BLACKWELL, ARON BONAR, SAM BREACH, SIMON BROWN, TRIPP BROWN, MARIO CAPELLARI, ZACHARY COLE, LINDY DE QUATTRO, NATASHA DEVAUD, RICHARD DUCKER, SIMON EVES, BRAD FALK, TIM FORTENBERRY, CHRISTIAN FOUCHER, RYAN GALLOWAY, WILLI GEIGER, BRANKO GRUJCIC, DAVID HISANAGA, PEG HUNTER, POLLY ING, SAMSON KAO, ED KRAMER, JOSHUA LEBEAU, DOUGLAS R. MACMILLAN, SCOTT MEASE, DAVID MENY, JOSEPH METTEN, MICHAEL MUIR, HENRY PRESTON, RICARDO RAMOS, DYLAN ROBINSON, AMANDA RONAI, ALAN ROSENFELD, JAMES ROWELL, ERIC TEXIER, MEGHAN THORNTON, BARBARA TOWNSEND, ROBERT WEAVER, KENNETH WESLEY

Animators ....CHARLES ALLENECK, STEVE APLIN, CHRISTOPHER ARMSTRONG, DERRICK CARLIN, SCOTT CARROLL, MARC CHU, JONATHEN COLLINS, RONALD FRIEDMAN, DAVID GAINEY, ROBERT GIANINO, MAIA KAYSER, PETER KELLY, LEONID LARIONOV, DAVID LATOUR, ALISON LEAF, VICTORIA LIVINGSTONE, JONATHAN LYONS, WESLEY MANDELL, KEVIN MARTEL, ROBERT MCINTOSH, PHILIP MCNALLY, CHRISTOPHER MITCHELL, PHILIP MORRIS, RICK O'CONNOR, MARK POWER, JASON RENNIE, MAGALI RIGAUDIAS, THOMAS ST. AMAND, DELIO TRAMONTOZZI, MARJOLAINE TREMBLAY-SILVA, JAN VAN BUYTEN, DAVID WEINSTEIN, ANDY WONG, DANIEL ZIZMOR
Technical Animators ....ANDY BUECKER, BRADLEY GABE, CHRISTOPHER MONKS, JEFF WHITE, JOHN ZDANKIEWICZ
Motion Capture Lead ....DOUG GRIFFIN
Motion Capture Technicians..........MICHAEL SANDERS KEVIN WOOLEY
Lead Compositors ....TODD VAZIRI, BRIAN CONNOR, FRANCOIS LAMBERT
Compositors ....JON ALEXANDER, LEAH ANTON, JOEL BEHRENS, MATT BRUMIT, DON CRAWFORD, SCOTT DAVID, DAVID DEUBER, SAM EDWARDS, BILL EYLER, ANGELA GIANNONI, NATHALIE GIRARD, KELLY GRANITE, SHERRY HITCH, HEATHER HOYLAND, MICHAEL JAMIESON, MICHAEL KENNEDY, STEPHEN KENNEDY, SIOBHAN LO, KRISTEN MILLETTE, ARRY SAFLEY, GREG SALTER, KEN SJOGREN, SHARMISHTHA SOHONI, RUSS SUEYOSHI, GUERDON TRUEBLOOD, SCOTT YOUNKIN
Sabre Artists ....CAITLIN CONTENT, ADAM HOWARD, KEVIN MAY, SEBASTIEN MOREAU, CHAD TAYLOR, ALEX TROPIEC, RITA ZIMMERMAN
VFX Location Coordinator............WAYNE BILLHEIMER
VFX Coordinators ....NINA FALLON, GLENN KARPF, GORDON WITTMANN, JILL HUGHES, LAURA DENICKE, SARAH PEACOCK, LORI ARNOLD
Digital Modelers................................KENNETH BRYAN, PAMELA CHOY, JACK HAYE, JUNG-SEUNG HONG, YIU-YUN HSIEH, LANA LAN, LENNY LEE, ALYSON MARKELL, GIOVANNI NAKPIL, MAURICE NOVEMBRE, MARK SIEGEL, HONG SUCK SUH, OMAR VELASCO
Viewpaint Artists ....LEIGH BARBIER, CATHERINE CRAIG, BRIDGET GOODMAN, REBECCA HESKES, DONNA TENNIS
Lead Creature TDs ....KEIJI YAMAGUCHI, LEE UREN, ANDREA MAIOLO, HIROMI ONO, ANDREW ANDERSON, ERIC WONG, TIM BRAKENSIEK
Creature TDs..................................KENNETH BAILEY, JEFFREY BERNSTEIN, KATHLEEN DAVIDSON, KARIN DERLICH, LIOUDMILA GOLYNSKAIA, SUNNY LEE, VIJAY MYNENI, SABA ROUFCHAIE, JASON SMITH, RENITA TAYLOR, GREG WEINER
Location Matchmovers ....JOHN WHISNANT THOMAS BURNETTE
CG Layout Artists ....ALIA AGHA, COLIN BENOIT, DUNCAN BLACKMAN, LANNY CERMAK, LYDIA CHOY, RAY GILBERTI, MARIA GOODALE, WENDY HENDRICKSON-ELLIS, WOONAM KIM, JOSHUA LIVINGSTON, JODIE MAIER, DANI MORROW, P. JEEP NAARKOM, JESSE RADEMACHER, JEFFREY SALTZMAN,

JAMES SOUKUP, PATRICK TURNER, DAVID WASHBURN, TALMAGE WATSON, ROLAND YEPEZ
Digital Matte Artists ....RICHARD BLUFF, TOSHIYUKI MAEDA, YUSEI UESUGI, WEI ZHENG
Lead Digital Paint / Roto Artist ....JIRI JACKNOWITZ
Digital Paint / Rotoscope Artists ....CHRIS BAYZ, HUGH BENGS, ERIC CHRISTENSEN, LEE CROFT, NIKA DUNNE, DAN FEINSTEIN, AIDAN FRASER, DAWN GATES, CAM GRIFFIN, TREVOR HAZEL, PATRICK JARVIS, SARAHJANE JAVELO, DREW KLAUSNER, JENNIFER MACKENZIE, JAKE MAYMUDES, REGAN MCGEE, LAUREN MORIMOTO, AMY SHEPARD, M. ZACHARY SHERMAN, ALAN TRAVIS, ERIN WEST, HEIDI ZABIT
ATDs................DAVID HIRSCHFIELD, MICHAEL RICH
Research & Development ....DAVID BULLOCK, MAX CHEN, ZORAN KACIC-ALESIC, RYAN KAUTZMAN, TONY PELLE, PHIL PETERSON, CARY PHILLIPS, NICO POPRAVKA, ARI RAPKIN, RITO TREVINO
VFX Director of Photography.....MARTIN ROSENBERG
Model Shop Supervisor ....MICHAEL LYNCH
Stage Production Manager ....MONIQUE GOUGEON-DI COMO
Model Makers ....LAUREN ABRAMS, CHARLES BAILEY, TORI BELLECI, DONALD BIES, ROBERT EDWARDS, STEPHEN GAWLEY, JON GUIDINGER, NELSON HALL, GRANT IMAHARA, ERIK JENSEN, TODD LOOKINLAND, RICHARD MILLER, DAVID MURPHY, RANDY OTTENBERG, LORNE PETERSON, THOMAS PROOST, MARK WALAS
Assistant Camera Operator ....ROBERT HILL
Stage Support...BILL BARR, BERNIE DEMOLSKI, MICHAEL OLAGUE
Practical FX Supervisor ....GEOFF HERON
Practical FX Foreman............................ROBBIE CLOT
Visual FX Editorial............................CAREY BURENS, LARRY HOKI, NICHOLAS PROVENZANO
VFX Production Assistants.CHRISTINE CASTELLANO, KATHERINE FARRAR, MILLIE LI
Production &Technical Support ....DAVID BURNCE, KAI CHANG, GRANTLAND GEARS, C. ALLEN GILES, AUDRA KOKLYS, MARK MARCIN, MARC OSTROFF, DAVID YEE
Digital Imaging Operators ....ANDREA BIKLIAN, RICHARD GENTNER, DARREN JONES
Technical & Computer Support ....CHRIS FOREMAN, RYAN JONES, EMILY KLUCZYNSKI, DAVID NAHMAN-RAMOS, NEIL ROBINSON
Visual Effects Executive Producer .....JUDITH WEAVER
ILM Senior Staff ....JIM MORRIS, CHRISSIE ENGLAND, CLIFF PLUMER

Special Visual Effects by
SYD DUTTON and BILL TAYLOR, ASC
ILLUSION ARTS, INC.

Visual Effect Producer ....CATHERINE SUDOLCAN
Matte Painting Supervisor ....KELVIN MCILWAIN
Matte Artists............................JUSTIN BRANDSTATER, BOB SCIFO, ROCCO GIOFRE, ALP ALTINER
Lead Animator ....FUMI MASHIMO
Compositing ....DAVID S. WILLIAMS, JR., ADAM KOWALSKI, PATRICK MULANE, MATT HARTLE, NICK ILYIN, RICARDO TORRES
3-D Artists ....MICHAEL KORY, ANDREW TUCKER, MARY MANNING, MICHAEL MEYERS
Digital Supervisor......................RICHARD PATTERSON
Roto...MARK KENASTON

Visual Effects Coordinator ....COLLIN FOWLER
Special Rigging ....LYNN LEDGERWOOD
Visual Effects Editor ....MICHELE ROTHBURGH
Digital Assistant ....AARON SNOW

Visual Effects by WETA DIGITAL LTD.
Wellington, New Zealand
Visual Effects Supervisor ....JOE LETTERI
Visual Effects Exec. Producer ....EILEEN MORAN
Visual Effects Producer...............ANNETTE WULLEMS
CG Supervisor ....DAN LEMMON
2D Sequence Supervisor ....CHARLES TAIT
Senior Compositors ....SONIA CALVERT,
MASAKI MITCHELL, FRANK RUETER,
MATT WELFORD
3D Effects Lighting TD...........................SAM BUI
Massive Supervisor ....JON ALLITT
Visual Effects Coordinator ....MARVYN YOUNG
VFX Cinematographer ....BRIAN VAN'T HUL
Senior Matte Painter ....DYLAN COLE
Miniature Ship by ....WETA WORKSHOP

Visual Effects by DIGISCOPE LLC
Executive Producer ....MARY STUART WELCH
Compositing Supervisor...............BRENNAN PREVATT
Digital Artist ....TRAVIS BAUMANN
Digital Imaging Supervisor ....ADAM STARK
Visual Effects Producer ....LAUREL SCHULMAN

Visual Effects by PACIFIC TITLE & ARTS STUDIO
Visual Effects Supervisor ....MARK FREUND
Compositors ....CRAIG MATHIESON,
JENNIFER LAW-STUMP, TOM LAMB
3D Technical Supervisor ....JOE FRANCIS

Visual Effects by ZOIC STUDIOS, INC.
Executive Producer...........................LONI PERISTERE
Visual Effects Supervisor ....CHRISTOPHER JONES
CG Supervisor ....ANDREW ORLOFF
Visual Effects Producer ....KRISTEN LEIGH BRANAN
3D Animator...DAVE FUNSTON

Visual Effects by CIS HOLLYWOOD
Visual Effects Supervisor ....GREG LIEGEY
Visual Effects Producer ....JULIE OROSZ
Lead Compositor ....MARC NANJO
Lead CG Artist ....CHRISTOPHER RYAN
Roto/Paint Artist ....JAYNI KAVANAUGH

Additional Visual Effects..................BUF, COBALT FX,
HOWARD ANDERSON COMPANY, YU+CO, INC.,
PERPETUAL MOTION PICTURES
Additional Previsualization PIXEL LIBERATION FRONT

Production Services in the
Czech Republic Provided by ....STILLKING FILMS
Associate Producers
for Stillking Films ....MATTHEW STILLMAN
DAVID MINKOWSKI

PRAGUE UNIT
Production Supervisor ....LYNN ANDREWS
Production Manager............................JANA HRBKOVA
First Assistant Director ....MIREK LUX
Art Director.......................................JAROMIR SVARC
Assistant Art Director ....MARTIN VACKAR
Assistant Set Decorator ....BARA BUCHAROVA
Set Decorating P.A. ....FRANTISEK COPF
Draftsman...PAVEL TATAR
Dressing Supervisor ....JOHN WELLS
Supervising Standby ....ROBERT HILL
Props Storeman ....DAVID CHEESMAN
Propmaker ....DUNCAN MCDEVITT

Dressing Charge Hand ....KEITH VOWELS
Property Coordinator...........................BARA BAROVA
Leadman...JAN KODERA
Prop Buyer ....HONZA HOFFMANN
Prop Standby ....LUKAS LEHOUCKA,
JIRI NAVRATIL, ZBYNEK VIT
1st Assistant B Camera ....JOSEPH PONTICELLE
2nd Assistant B Camera ....ZDENEK MRKVICKA
C Camera Operator ....KLAUS FUXJAGER
1st Assistant C Camera ....FRANTISEK NOVAK
2nd Assistant C Camera ....JAN VOJTECH
Video Assist Operator ....VIKTOR LONEK
Video Assistant ....KAREL SCHNEIBERG
Boom Operator ....ANDREW GRIFFITH
Cableman...JAN SKALA
Production Coordinators............JENNIFER GILLESPIE
KATKA SILNA
Assistant Coordinator...................LENKA KADLECOVA
Production Secretary.......................LENKA PAVLAKOVA
2nd Assistant Director ....MARTIN SEBIK
2nd 2nd Assistant Director .....MARTINA GOTTHANSOVA
3rd Assistant Director.............DAVID STRANGMULLER
Gaffer ....ONDREJ ARNAUTOV
Best Boy Electric ....BOREK KLECKA
Rigging Gaffer..................JEFFREY P. SODERBERG
Rigging Gaffers...........PAVEL CASLAVSKY, MIRO ZILA
Rigging Best Boys Electric................VACLAV KORCIK,
IGOR MURCO
Key Grip ....JIRI GAZDA
Dolly Grip ....KAREL CHARVAT
Best Boy Rigging Grip...............EKKEHARD BOEHNEL
Special Effects Foremen ....STEVE CREMIN
DAVID HERON
Special Effects Sr. Technician .....ONDREJ NIEROSTEK
Special Effects Technicians...............GARRY COOPER,
ANTE DUGANDZIC, CHRISTIAN EUBANK,
STEVEN FICKE, MARK GULLESSERIAN,
THOMAS R. HOMSHER, GARTH INNS, NICK KARAS,
WILLIAM D. KENNEDY, JOE KLEIN, TOM KNOTT,
WILLIAM LEE, DARREN MAY, ED REIFF,
ALAN RIFKIN, MICHAEL RIFKIN,
CHRISTOPHER SUAREZ, GLENN THOMAS,
TOM TOKUNAGA, ANDREW WEDER,
OUGLAS ZIEGLER, MILOS BROSSINGER,
MIROSLAV MICLIK, VACLAV MORAVEC,
JAN MORO, KAREL SEBL, STANISLAV SMERAL,
KAREL SOLC, BORIS TATAROV,
RUDOLF TUDZAROFF, JAKUB WUDY
Key Makeup Artist.......................................JIRI FARKAS
Key Hair Stylist ....JANA RADILOVA
Location Manager ....PAVEL MRKOUS
Location Consultant ....PAUL PAV
Assistant Location Manager ....PETR SKVOR
On Set Location Manager ....PAVEL VORACEK
Accountant ....VERA TROUSILOVA
Assistant Accountants ....IVA LUKESOVA,
MARCELA SOLDATOVA, MICHAL ENGRTH
Head Horse Master ....STEVE DENT
Key Horse Masters...........................JIM LOCKWOOD
MIKE BOYLE
Casting ....NANCY BISHOP
Extras Casting ....EXTRAFILMS
Production Office Assistants ....MARTIN CIGLER,
SILVIA JANCULOVA
Key Set P.A. ....LUKAS LIBAL
Set Production Assistant................LUCIE BURIANOVA
Art Department Coordinator .....MARKETA PUZMANOVA
Art Department P.A. ....MICHAL SMID
Transportation Coordinator ....GUSTAFF HUSAK
Construction Coordinator ....RAY BARRETT
Lead Scenics ....DAVID MEEKING, DAVID MEARS
Standby Construction ....PAVEL WERNER,
DALIBOR TVRZNIK

Standby Painter ....JAKUB BERDYCH
Specialty Painter ....STUART JAMES CLARKE
Painter ....BARBORA RUZICKOVA
Cablecam Key ....JAMES RODUNSKY
Cablecam Operator ....ALEX MACDONALD
Caterers.............JTV CATERING, TOMAS JESETICKY
Stunt Coordinator ....MARTIN HUB

Stunts ....PAVEL BEZDEK, RUDOLF BOK,
PETR BOZDECH, VIKTOR CERVENKA,
FRANTISEK DEAK, ZUZANA DRDACKA,
HANA DVORSKA, MICHAL GRUN, RENE HAJEK,
ROMANA HAJKOVA, ANTON HAUSKNECHT,
PETR HNETKOVKSY, JAN HOLICEK,
PETR HORACEK, IRI HORKY, EDA HUBATA,
LANKA JAROSOVA, FILIP KADLEC,
JINDRICH KLAUS, ALES KOSNAR, JIRI KRAUS,
ROBERT KREJCIK, MILOS KULHAVY,
ROBERT LAHODA, LADISLAV LAHODA, MIROSLAV
LHOTKA, DIMO LIPITKOVSKY,
DAVID LISTVAN, IVAN MARES,
KLARA MORAVKOVA, DAVID MOTTL,
PAVEL MYSLIK, MIROSLAV NAVRATIL,
VACLAV PACAL, TOMAS PETERAC,
JAROSLAV PETERKA, JAN PETRINA,
JAROSLAV PSENICKA, ALES PUTIKK,
PETR SEKANINA, JIRI SIMBERSKY,
KLARA SLAVIKOVA, MILAN SLEPICKA,
STADHERR, TOMAS TOBOLA, MIROSLAV VALKA,
KAREL VAVROVEC, PETR VLASAK,
PAVEL VOKOUN, JAN VOSMIK,
KAMILA ZENKEROVA

2nd Unit
First Assistant Director ...CHRISTIAN P. DELLA PENNA
Second Assistant Director....................KEVIN DUNCAN
Assistant Production
Coordinator ....MATTHEW LEONETTI, JR
Director of Photography....................JOSH BLEIBTREU
Script Supervisor.................................HALEY McLANE
Stunt Coordinator ....TROY BROWN

2nd Unit – Los Angeles
Camera Operator ....DAVID LUKENBACH
1st Assistant A Camera ....STEVE PETERSON
2nd Assistant A Camera....................RON PETERSON
B Camera Operator ....LEO NAPOLITANO
1st Assistant B Camera ....MIKE FAUNTLEROY
2nd Assistant B Camera ....JAY C. HAGER
Camera Loader ....MATTHEW A. DEL RUTH
Libra Technician...JOHN BONNIN
Video Assist ....SAM R. HARRISON III
Gaffer ....GARY TANDROW
Best Boy Electric.............................GEORGE LOZANO
Key Grip ....BEN BEAIRD
Best Boy Grip ....KEVIN FITZGERALD
Dolly Grips...JEFF KUNKEL
STEVE ROBERTSON
Sound Mixer ....SUSUMU TOKUNOW
Boom Operators ....DOUG SHAMBURGER
CHRISTOPHER DIAMOND
Set Production Assistants ....JOSH ERNSTROM
CRAIG GLENN
Caterer ....THOMAS LINDLEY
Craft Service..MARIA NUNEZ

2nd Unit – Prague
Production Supervisor ....JIM SCAIFE
Unit Manager ....PAVEL TYPOLT
First Assistant Director...........................JAN MENSIK
On Set Dresser ....MICHAL SVOBODA
Camera Operators.............IAN FOX, MILAN CHADIMA

CREDITS

1st Assistant A Camera ....ZORAN VESELIC
2nd Assistant A Camera ....TOMAS MUNZPERGER
B Camera Operator............................ERVIN SANDERS
1st Assistant B Camera ....LADISLAV HRUBY
2nd Assistant B Camera.................PETR MACHACEK
Production Sound Mixer ....PETR FOREJT
Boom Operator.......................................ROMAN RIGO
Production Coordinator ....JANA VESELA
Assistant Coordinator..........................BOBAN DVORAK
2nd 2nd Assistant Directors ....LUBOS KADANE,
JAKUB DVORAK
Gaffers...............PATRICK REDDISH, PETR KONRAD
Best Boy Electric ....PETR BERTA SULC
Rigging Gaffers ....WERNER SCHELZIG
VLADIMIR HOLZKNECHT
Key Grips ....WILLIAM PATSOS,
MARK SANNES, ROMAN HODEK
Best Boy Grips ....KEITH BUNTING, MILOS KABELA
Grips ....DAN HAVELKA,
JIRI VOJTA HOVORKA, JAN KOVARIK
Special Effects Set Supervisor..........DAVID BLITSTEIN
Special Effects Set Foreman................PAVEL SAGNER
Costume Supervisor ....LINDSAY PUGH
Set Costumers ....MARIE CHARVATOVA,
JACKIE CHENG, ROSSANO MARCHI,
JITKA SVECOVA, VIERA ZVONAROVA
Key Makeup Artist...................................MILAN VLCEK
Key Hair Stylists ....JERI BAKER
IVANA NEMCOVA
Location Manager ....ANETA VALASKOVA
Assistant Location Managers ....JAKUB EXNER
JAN SVOBODA
Location Assistant............................MAREK SEDLARIK
Key Set Production Assistants ....JUSTIN SALEM
OLDRICH PRUSA
Set Production Assistants ....PETRA GOLDSMIDOVA,
STEPAN FARKAS, MICHAL MOTYCKA
Extras Coordinator.........................DUSAN ROBOVSKY
Transportation Coordinator......................EFFA KOTLAS
Standby Construction ....MIROSLAV MRAZ
VLADIMIR PRIBYSLAVSKY
Standby Painter ....VACLAV HENDRYCH
Caterers ....KUCA CATERING
JTV CATERING

Executive in Charge of Music for
Universal Pictures ....KATHY NELSON
Supervising Music Editor ....KENNETH KARMAN
Music Editor...JOHN FINKLEA
Assistant Music Editor.................JACQUELINE TAGER
Apprentice Music Editor............................BEN SCHOR

Orchestrations ....MARK MCKENZIE
Additional Orchestrations ....WILLIAM ROSS,
DAVID SLONAKER
Music Recorded & Mixed by ....DENNIS SANDS
Orchestra Contractor................SANDY DECRESCENT
Music Preparation ....JOANN KANE MUSIC SERVICE
Hollywood Film Chorale.....................SALLY STEVENS
Score Recorded at ....SONY PICTURES
SCORING STAGE
Recordist..ADAM MICHALAK
Score Technician ....PAT WEBER
Programmer...DAVID BIFANO

Title Design ..............KALEIDOSCOPE FILMS GROUP
Opticals ....HOWARD ANDERSON
Negative Cutter ....BUENA VISTA NEGATIVE CUTTING

Digital Intermediate by EFILM

Digital Color Timer............................STEVEN J. SCOTT
Digital Intermediate Producer ....TERRA BLISS
Digital Intermediate Editor ....NATHAN FITZGERALD
Digital Colorist Assist ....NTANA B. KEY
Scanning/Recording Manager ....WAYNE ADAMS
Digital Intermediate Coordinator ....HELGA SALMENA

Camera Dollies by ....CHAPMAN / LEONARD
STUDIO EQUIPMENT, INC.
Remote Cranes & Heads..........PANAVISION REMOTE
SYSTEMS
Lighting & Grip Equipment......................ARRI RENTAL

SOUNDTRACK ON DECCA / UMG SOUNDTRACKS

The Filmmakers Wish to Thank:
Prague City Hall
City District of Prague 1;. Pavel Vlach, Karel Zrout
City District of Prague - Kunratice; Ivana Kabelova,
Vaclav Chalupa
National Museum- Department of Entomology,
Kunratice
Archbishopic Palace of Prague; Karel Sticha,
Marek Cihar
Prague Castle; Frantise Kadlec
City of Tabor
Hussite Museum Tabor; Phdr. Milos Drda, Petr Bratka
Institute of Botany, Academy of Sciences
of The Czech Republic
Administration of the Park of Pruhonice;. Ivan Stana
National Institute for the Preservation of Cultural
Heritage – Pernstein Castle
J.M. Schlick Kontinuum – Prachov Rocks

Chko - Protected Landscape Areas –
Cesky Raj & Cesky Kras
Czech Universtiy of Agriculture at Prague
The Forest Establishment at Kostelec Nad Cernymi
Lesy – Jevany Forest
Forest of the Czech Republic, State Enterprise Hradec
Kralove
Forest District – Tabor
Academy of Performing Arts – Faculty of Music
Department of City Parks – Hvezda
City District of Prague 6
Ministry of the Environment of the Czech Republic
Playa Vista Land Development Co.
Larry Butler Electrical Inc.
Moreno Valley Construction
AE Schmidt Company
Los Angeles Fire Dept. – Film Desk –
Fire Capt. Larry Shipp
City of Downey - Economic Development Office
City of Downey Fire Dept. - Deputy Chief Robert L.
Rowe, Asst. Chief Chuck Seely
City of Palos Verdes City Hall - Film Office
City of Palos Verdes Parks and Recreation Dept.

American Humane Association monitored
the animal action. No animal was harmed
in the making of this film.

FILMED WITH PANAVISION CAMERAS AND LENSES

Color by TECHNICOLOR

ACKNOWLEDGMENTS

The publisher wishes to thank the following for their special contributions to the creation of this book:
Guy Adan, Dawn Ahrens, Melissa Amador, Veronika Beltran, Kevin Campbell, Cindy Chang, Bob Ducsay,
Syd Dutton, Eddie Egan, Bette Einbinder, Colleen Foster, Elizabeth Gelfand, Illusion Arts, Industrial Light + Magic,
Darryl Maxwell, David O'Connor, Miles Perkins, Jennifer Sandberg, Scott Squires, Stephen Sommers, Matthew Stuecken,
and Universal Studios.